Management of Archives and Manuscript Collections for Librarians

Richard H. Lytle
Editor

Published by The Society of American Archivists
1980

Reprinted from the *Drexel Library Quarterly*,
January 1975, Vol. 11, No. 1

Contents

Editor's Note

The original printing of *Management of Archives and Manuscript Collections for Librarians,* which appeared in mid-1975, sold out within six months. The editorial offices of the *Drexel Library Quarterly* have received continuing demand for copies over the past four years, and I have received a number of personal requests to have the issue reprinted. The present reprinting is done with the cooperation of Dr. Guy G. Garrison, Dean of the Drexel University School of Library and Information Science, and Ms. Barbara Casini, editor of the *Drexel Library Quarterly.* I want to express my appreciation for their cooperation.

This reprinting contains no changes in the body text of the articles. The cover and title pages have been changed and this preface has been added. Passage of the 1976 copyright act renders obsolete some of the observations of Dr. Cox's article, "The Law and the Manuscripts Curator," and that has been noted at the beginning of that article. The reader is reminded that the selective bibliography was prepared in 1974.

Readers should note a very important addition to the literature since 1975; the Society of American Archivists' Basic Manual Series. These publications are listed on the back cover of the volume.

Richard H. Lytle
Smithsonian Institution Archives
February 1980

Preface

Several years ago, a well-known scholar appeared at the doors of one of the East's most distinguished research libraries. He asked for the manuscripts curator, and then asked to see one of the manuscript collections. He wanted to be admitted to the stacks. The curator responded that researchers could not browse in the collection, but rather that collections were brought out a few boxes at a time. No, he wanted to *see* the collection as it was placed in the stacks, but he did not wish to go through it at the moment. Bewildered, the curator agreed—he knew this historian by his considerable reputation—and the man spent some time looking at the collection on the shelves and taking a few notes, but he never opened a box. He returned to the reading room, talked briefly with a young man who had accompanied him, and came back to the curator. He was ready for lunch, and asked where he might eat. Upon returning from lunch, he again asked to see the collection on the shelves. By this time the curator was throughly annoyed, but he was also very curious, and thus permitted bending of the rules a second time. The researcher looked at the collection and by some inscrutable selection process indicated boxes on the shelves to be taken to the reading room. He then took notes, obviously knowing just where to look within each box. After a time, he returned the boxes to the curator, announced the success of his inquiry, and prepared to leave. The curator, quite beside himself now, asked the historian how he had made his search. "Oh," he replied, "the young man who accompanied me is a medium, and he told me where to look in the collection for what I wanted."

Perhaps every research library should have a medium to assist researchers; and if a person with such powers were available, doubtless he would spend much of his time among the archives and manuscript collections. For these sources, if not really mysterious, often appear so to librarians accustomed to a more ordered world of physical location and information retrieval. Since this issue of the *Drexel Library Quarterly* is directed toward librarians who have archival responsibilities but little archival training or experience, a brief comparison of archives and books is pertinent.

The major difference between librarians and archivists is cosmic —a difference in world view. Archivists accept the organizational structure of their resources and interpret this order to users. Librarians, on the other hand, impose an order on their materials through comprehensive structures for organization of knowledge. From the librarian's viewpoint, the archivist's world is a patchwork of conflicting systems, not nearly so neat as the structure resulting from classification.

The assumptions and techniques of archivist and librarian derive from this fundamental difference in the nature of books and archives. Archives usually come to the curator with an internal order imposed by their creators; unless the original order has been destroyed beyond recognition, it is preserved. There are two justifications for this archival principle. First, it is usually the only practical method for administering archives, since filing individual papers into a preconceived order is not within the staffing capabilities of most institutions. But more important, the original order itself has value; that is, the organization of archives is indispensable to full interpretation of the items within the archival body. For example, if a colleague places memoranda received from me in a special part of his records labeled "nut file," the context of this document will tell researchers as much or more than the actual information contained in the memoranda. More seriously, file structures often indicate how an institution or person organized his affairs, and may reveal relationships between subjects, activities and persons.

From another perspective, published matter may be said to be subject-oriented, while archives are source-oriented. Although source may be a complex matter for some publications, this is unusual and in any case a quite different problem than for archives. For the archivist, source may be more important than subject; or more likely, source may be the archivist's approach to subject. The archival concern for source, called *the principle of provenance,* and preservation of the original order comprise the two primary doctrines of archives administration.

It follows that organization of archival bodies within archival institutions differs radically from the organization of books within libraries. A library's structure derives from a comprehensive sys-

Preface

tem for organizing knowledge which results, theoretically, at
least, in a coherent, rationalized arrangement of books on shelves
and cards in catalogs. Archives, on the contrary, consist of a
multitude of structures—created by many different offices and
persons over many years—preserved intact by archivists. Some
archival establishments arrange archival units on shelves by
source (office of creation), while others use an arbitrary numbering system which places archival units on shelves in order of
receipt. All good archives programs preserve a record of the organizational or personal sources of their materials. No experienced archivist attempts to set up his physical location arrangement by subject, for the obvious reason that most archival units
will relate to many subjects and, as already shown, archivists do
not disturb the original order of archives for subject or other
rearrangements.

If the physical arrangement of materials within an archives appears rather unorganized to librarians, information retrieval techniques appear downright chaotic. Scholars tend to approach archival resources with less structured questions than those with
which they approach general book collections; or at least, I suspect that this is so. In any case, the archivist has less structure
upon which to rely for response. An archivist servicing the archives of an institution converts subject questions into source
questions; that is, he asks himself what administrative division
would have executed business related to that topic and then he
searches the archives of that division. The archivist must know
the administrative history of his institution, in the light of which he
identifies "likely" or "possible" units whose archives might pertain to the subject question at hand. Even when the archivist
creates aids for searching the archives, the user ultimately relies
upon the inherent structure of the archives. In libraries which
collect archives and manuscript collections, a very similar process may be used to guide the researcher to the sources.

Yet another important factor distinguishes archives administration from librarianship. The archivist's decision to retain or dis-
card archives—or the manuscript curator's determination of what
to collect—is quite different from the librarian's development of
book acquisition policy. Because each archival body is unique,
the archivist determines what will be retained for posterity, and
this judgment requires a thorough knowledge of his institution
and relevant subject areas, and seasoned perception of the research potential of archives. This function—called *records*

Preface

appraisal—is the most important aspect of the profession of archives administration. Although records appraisal requires a perspective on information needs not unlike that acquired by a librarian building a book collection, the activities are in fact quite different.

If this issue has a major theme, it is the importance of setting priorities. Rational priorities are necessary for even the smallest program. The first priority should be to define a rational collecting program, to gain elementary control over all archives/manuscript materials, and to communicate knowledge of holdings to the scholarly community; this is really a single priority in that the whole program must be planned and regulated so that usable collections are made available to scholars. Many topics are discussed, but the priorities theme will be noted throughout the issue.

The issue consists of eight articles. The first, by Paul McCarthy, provides an overview of establishing and administering an archives or manuscripts program. The second article, by Mary Lynn McCree, discusses problems of defining manuscript collections and the actual business of collecting. The two following articles deal with processing manuscripts; Richard Berner discusses processing manuscript collections, and Ralph Ehrenberg discusses problems of processing and handling of aural and graphic archives. Henry Bartholomew Cox provides an introduction to the manuscript curator's legal problems, and Clark Nelson discusses preservation. The last topical article, by Robert Rosenthal, perhaps should be the first, since it discusses the goal of all archival/manuscript operations: the use of the repository's resources. Frank Evan's bibliographical essay concludes the issue.

The reader is advised to glance over the appendix on terminology before reading the issue, paying especial attention to the initial section on use of the terms *archives* and *manuscript collections*.

The editor and contributors hope to make a practical contribution which will be useful for librarians who have archival responsibilities.

Richard H. Lytle
Archivist
Smithsonian Institution
Washington, D.C.

Overview: Essentials of an Archives or Manuscripts Program

Paul H. McCarthy, Jr.

Managing a small institutional archives or manuscript depository can be an exciting, intellectually stimulating and emotionally rewarding experience if the program fulfills real needs, is well managed, and is utilized and appreciated by its public. If you have had a major share in shaping and administering that program, the work can be professionally satisfying indeed.

Since this issue is directed primarily to those persons who have a part-time responsibility for archives and manuscripts or who are taking up this responsibility for the first time, this article will give a general overview of the management of the small archives or manuscript program. Considerations important to the program, general procedures, program development and the responsibilities, opportunities and problems involved in a program will be outlined in this article, with more important aspects discussed in greater detail by subsequent authors.

Initial Considerations

The time to outline the expectations for a program and the criteria by which it is to be judged is at the outset. The primary question any administrator, librarian or archivist should raise is "will the program fulfill a real need, or will it be offering a service that is already provided by another institution or organization in better facilities with a more competent staff?" The analysis of real needs and the appraisal of the institution's capabilities of fulfilling these needs should be primary considerations. These should be thoroughly discussed and evaluated before an institution commits its resources to an archival or manuscript program.

A viable program must fulfill real needs for the community it serves, be that community a group of scholars investigating historical problems, administrators utilizing archives for management decisions, scientists gathering notes from historical observations or local historians or genealogists researching their communities and families. Besides fulfilling real needs for its community, an archival or manuscript program must have a definite focus or collecting theme, institutional support and understanding of its specialized needs, and a skilled staff and adequate facilities for the preservation of its resources.

The kind of public it expects to serve should have an extremely important part in determining the focus of a manuscript program. A resident population of scholars, be they academic or lay, vitally interested in extensive collections of personal papers or archives demand different kinds of collections and different services than the more casual users, primarily interested in historical documentation of local counties, towns or families. The first group may wish the institution to acquire extensive collections which would be useful for in-depth studies, while the second type of user may be more interested in documentation relating to important municipal developments and family genealogies or photographic files which visually preserve the area's past.

The focus or collecting themes of each institution are as individual and unique as the institution itself. Broadly speaking, however, the principal themes might well be broken down into geographical, family or business collections that might be of interest to a county historical society; particular subjects (i.e., the records of labor unions); a defined chronological period (i.e., records relating to the Revolutionary War); or specific types of records (i.e., business records).

The process of establishing collecting themes for the manuscript program is a process of establishing the needs of the community and its researchers and also the time for a careful and critical assessment of the manuscript resources available to the proposed program. Perceptive staff members should be able to estimate, at least in general terms, the likelihood of carrying out the collecting themes. Collecting themes, like goals, tend to be optimistic. Much healthy skepticism is in order for a frank appraisal of the possible success of the program.

An institution should build on its strength, its public's needs and the resources available to it. Small institutions beginning new programs are ill-advised to duplicate the efforts of already established, well-run programs. Institutions should avoid soliciting collections of records from other institutions that already have good archival programs.

Overview

Once the considerations, themes, researcher needs and historical resources available are well on their way to being defined, the institution must squarely face what may well be the most limiting factor: cost.

Financial Implications

The costs involved in running a viable manuscript or archival program are significant, even for small programs with volunteer help. Poorly or inadequately supported programs have a debilitating effect on staff morale, on the institution's image, and most important, on the use of historical materials. It is necessary to balance the positive reasons for implementing a program with a very realistic appraisal of the costs of acquisition of materials, maintenance of facilities and staff time for processing and reference service. There are no free gifts! Collections, even those given freely, cost staff time and money to acquire. Certainly the institution incurs major ethical and financial responsibilities when it accepts collections to arrange, describe, preserve and make available for research use.

Facilities are expensive, not only when new buildings are constructed or old buildings are refurbished, but also when only daily maintenance and upkeep are required. While this may be of direct concern only if the program or its governing agency has the immediate responsibility for construction and maintenance of its own facilities, facilities always cost money. Archival and manuscript programs must justify the value of their programs in competition with other agencies or departments for the same space and dollars. It is important to have a realistic idea of the implications and demands that programs make on facilities and budgets in evaluating or reevaluating programs. An understanding of direct and indirect costs can be of great assistance in comprehending total program costs.

Staff costs appear as a significant portion of any budget. Salaries, while they comprise most of the staff costs, are by no means all of them. Only when salaries are coupled with fringe benefits, employer contributions, insurance, payroll costs and non-program facilities needed for staff can one begin to arrive at an accurate estimate of staff costs.

Expenditures for equipment and supplies are costs often over-

Overview

looked by administrators or faculty as they consider implementing an archival or manuscript program. Besides the materials needed for routine office work, the program will need specialized supplies, such as acid-free file folders, archival boxes and rag board. While not considered a major portion of the budget, these and other expenses, such as travel, services, postage and freight, do form a significant addition.

Budgeting

The only way staffing and funding of archives and manuscript repositories have a competitive chance is if the program is important to the institution and the effects of the program are demonstrable. Sound budgeting is critical to gaining support for a program. A detailed budget must lay out all the expected expenses in categories of personnel services, purchases of collections (if appropriate), travel, equipment and supplies. Once the principal functions of the program have been outlined, the estimates of staff time required for each function can be made.

Staff time estimates for each function can then be "costed out" in terms of direct and indirect costs. In most cases the budget will be justified with reference to work (i.e., the collections it will bring in, arrange and describe) and effectiveness (i.e., types and numbers of researchers utilizing collections). Program budgeting —measurement of inputs and outputs and analysis of program effectiveness—can be painful and agonizing, but will pay off in funds if executed effectively.

The budgetary process also provides an opportunity to reflect on the present and future capabilities of the program. It should provide a prospectus of what is possible and guide the institution to undertake only what it has a reasonably good chance of doing well. The institution must be continually aware of the finite nature of its resources and must balance its resources against demands and requirements of its program.

Staffing

Staffing poses different problems for small archives and manuscript repositories than for larger ones. Unless the situation is quite unusual, funds available for staff will never be sufficient to

Overview

recruit specialized personnel. The staff will have to be flexible enough to handle and enjoy a variety of assignments in both the technical and public facets.

A knowledge of the history of the community or subject, knowledge of archival procedures, accuracy, attention to detail and a willingness to work with the public are some of the personal characteristics of prospective staff which will be valuable to the program. Most smaller archives and manuscript repositories will be selecting staff from markets where few individuals will have any prior experience or training in archival work. They will have to select competent individuals who, with some formal or informal training, can be valuable assets. Informal, yet outlined, programs of in-house training and education, formal training in history (particularly local history) and other subjects related to the technical or subject aspects of the program will increase the pride and competence of staff members as well as the effectiveness of the program. A good source of training information is the newsletter of the Society of American Archivists.

Most smaller repositories find that clerical as well as professional staff have the opportunity to be involved in more of the program and can assume more responsibility than would be possible in a large program. This is a real advantage of a smaller program. Many smaller archives are also able to enlist volunteer help either on a permanent basis or for work on particular collections. With a limited budget, volunteers may allow the program longer hours of service and more time to arrange and describe collections. The capabilities of volunteer help and their commitment to the program ought to be assessed as critically as the capabilities and commitment of salaried staff members. Staff, whether paid or not, require training, facilities, equipment and supplies. It may be at least, if not more, difficult to regulate or terminate the services of volunteer help than paid staff.

A possible source of volunteer assistance is the local historical society membership or students in upper division work in history at a local college or university. Public and personal recognition of the individual volunteer's contributions to the program can make him or her feel an important part of the staff.

The staff members who are in the field representing the institution to its prospective donors occupy a key position. Their integrity must be beyond question. They must have a well-based knowledge of the needs of the program and its integral operations to convey the essence of the program to prospective donors. They must convince the donor of the importance of his or her papers, the reasons these papers should be preserved and available for research, but they must avoid making commitments to donors that the institution might not be able to honor. Larger institutions may assign this among several tasks to a single individual. Since these individuals represent the program to prospective donors and establish conditions of use and commitments on behalf of the institution, often serving as the only contact the donor has with the institution, they must be selected with great care.

An intellectual breadth and imagination are invaluable in staff charged with selecting materials to preserve in archives and manuscript collections. Changing perspectives, new ways of analyzing older materials and new emphasis in research all require the archivist to rethink the criteria used to judge the research value of materials.

Selection of Institutional Archives

The traditional criteria for evaluating records, particularly since the archivist has been hired by the institution to safeguard and preserve its own records, has been their administrative, legal, fiscal and historical value. Archives should preserve the significant records that document the institution's policies and procedures, the records documenting its legal establishment, operation and other records required by law, and its fiscal records, reflecting its financial operations. Public archives also have a very definite responsibility to preserve and make available those records that document the rights and prerogatives of their citizens. The historical utilization of archives has become increasingly significant, particularly in public institutions. Often, users approaching archives with what might be defined as a broadly-based historical point of view form a substantial percentage of all the users, as well as an influential base of support for these programs. The historical perspective is also very important to professional archivists. Few, if any, would have continued in the profession if archives were only concerned with administrative, legal and fiscal values.

The archivist must be familiar with the history and development of the institution he or she serves to gain a perspective as to what

records are of administrative, legal, fiscal or historical importance. While the archival experiences of similar institutions may
be of assistance in appraising the records of another, it is only
when those experiences are tempered with the unique history and
experiences of one's own institution that one can begin to establish a basis for an accurate appraisal, and thus selection of
records.

Once the significant records of the institution have been identified, procedures should be established to insure their orderly
retirement to the archives as they become noncurrent. The most
logical method is to establish disposition schedules covering all
of the institution's records; those of temporary value can be held
until no longer needed; those of long-term value can be retired to
assure their preservation. Disposition schedules are developed
after the records have been described as to type, purpose, period
covered, file order, frequency of use and value. The disposition of
the records should be established through the cooperative input
of the records creator, administrative and legal representatives,
records manager (if available), and the archivist. The disposition
schedules should be reviewed on a regular basis. Changing administrative needs and legal requirements and historical approaches may suggest that the schedules be amended.

While schedules and more formal evaluation procedures should
insure the preservation of significant records, archivists will always be involved in diplomatic negotiations with administrators
whose cooperation and understanding must be obtained if the
program is to be successful. In smaller institutions where administrators may feel especially protective of their records, the
person-to-person relationship between the creator of the records
and the archivist may assume paramount importance. The administrator, secretary or clerk must be assured that the records
will be as accessible as they have been in the past. With an efficient operation, the archivist will be able to assure him that, in
most cases, the records will be more easily available.

Selection of Manuscript Collections

Within the parameters of its collecting program and its themes,
the institution still has a variety of options by which to expand and
develop its programs. If the program is primarily geographic in
focus (i.e., county history), a basic knowledge of the history of the

community, its influential families and prominent industries is important. If the program emphasizes subject or chronological coverage, a basic knowledge of the subject, its important trends and leaders, is needed. A search of Hamer's *Guide to the Archives and Manuscripts of the United States* and the *National Union Catalog of Manuscript Collections* and a knowledge of the holdings of repositories with similar interests should indicate many of the sources that have already been tapped for collections.

Prospective donors can be contacted by a variety of techniques. An effective program will utilize a variety of means, such as individual conversations, letters, articles in local or subject publications, talks to local or professional groups, local radio or television discussion shows, to make its public aware of its purposes and its collecting themes. All these techniques are valuable and can help reinforce one another. Influential individuals in your community should be approached as well as organizations, such as the League of Women Voters, pioneer groups, Sierra clubs, chambers of commerce, if they fit within the collecting themes. In subject collections professional and lay groups active in the field should be solicited. Manuscript repositories should be wary in their approach to business records. Defunct businesses that helped shape the community may prove to have extremely significant records that document the community's development, but curators are well advised to be cautious about soliciting businesses whose records may overwhelm them. Some injudicious decisions may lead a local historical agency to becoming a de facto company archive, thus limiting its efforts to collect a broad range of community-related material.

While much of the program's efforts will be directed toward highly visible individuals and organizations, the repository also has an obligation to seek out materials that would document the experiences of lesser known and unknown individuals and groups. Too often material has been collected and history written that documents the few outstanding individuals or institutions of an age—an elitist history—while relatively little attention has been directed to the rest of the participants of the same era.

The range of types of materials to collect continues to expand. Manuscript collections, once the preserve of holograph materials, have expanded to include volumes of typescript letters and documents, historical photographs and films, computer printouts, oral tape recordings, and recently, videotape. Each of these forms can add unique and valuable information on the institution's collecting themes.

Accessioning

Once a donor has made a commitment to give papers or corporate or organizational records to the repository, most institutions provide assistance for transfer of materials and underwriting the costs of this transfer. This might be as simple as driving to the donor's house, packing the material and transporting it back to the institution, or it may involve contacting freight companies, arranging for the material to be packed, insured and forwarded on a collect basis. Some institutions have been fortunate enough to work with donors who not only are enthusiastic about placing their papers at an institution, but also realize the financial implication and have underwritten the transfer of material and the staff costs necessary to arrange and describe it. Such donors are rare.

The field representative or the individual doing the field work has the responsibility for alerting those in the repository that material is on its way. One of the benefits of a small staff is that more intimate working relationships allow most of the staff members to see the entire process, get a better feel for the program and participate in the arrangement, description and servicing of the collection. The participation in most facets of the work is quite different from traditional ways of handling library materials.

As material comes through either the front door in the hands of the donor or the receiving room door from the freight company, the staff has a responsibility to gain some kind of immediate intellectual control over the materials. The use of an accession register which serially numbers each and every discreet gift or transfer of discreet material to the archives or manuscript repository, as well as gathering other pertinent information about the gift or archival accession, is extremely important. The collections can be numbered using a system such as the date in combination with a unique number assigned serially to each discreet collection as it comes in. An example might be: the John H. Smith Papers, Accession #74-178. The accession number provides a key to the collection and also allows the repository the opportunity to develop files and keys to coordinate donors with collections and with accession numbers. Gifts should be accessioned immediately and the background material should include the title or subject of the collection, who gathered or created the collection (if it is not reflected in the title), who the donor is (with the appropriate address), and a very brief description of the papers.

During the initial inventory, a knowledgeable staff member should be on the alert, not only for the kinds of material involved, such as correspondence, financial records, scrapbooks, research files, etc., but also to assess the amount of time that may be needed to arrange and describe the collection. The time needed depends on the order of the collection, how well the materials are labeled, how carefully the collection has been packed, and what skills or knowledge the members of the processing staff have developed with similar collections. The physical condition of the records should also be assessed at this time. Specific recommendations, not only about the arrangement and description of the material, but comments on any particular parts of the collection that need special preservative techniques, can then be made. It is critically important for many manuscript repositories to appraise the physical condition of the records, particularly if they have no facility for fumigating incoming collections. Infested materials, once placed in a stack area, can prove to be very detrimental to the repository's entire holdings.

Certificate of Gift

Once the initial inventory is finished, a certificate of gift that legally transfers title to the collection should be prepared, noting any restrictions or exceptions to the conveyance of property rights and literary property rights, and forwarded to the donor for signature. This would also be the appropriate time for the staff members to remove the relevant correspondence relating to the donor, to transfer the material which in many repositories might be termed the "general correspondence" from the collection and place it in a collections file with a copy of the inventory. The collections file should contain all the correspondence relating to the collection, copies of legal deeds or certificates conveying the collection, publicity photographs of the donor or clippings and stories about the collection and other relevant material that would document the collection in the repository. Some repositories may wish to include any significant inquiries or correspondence relating to the collection with the collection file. However, with any volume of correspondence relating to the use of the collection, this arrangement would be impractical.

Once the inventory is complete, the formal acknowledgement of the gift to the donor along with the certificate of gift should be dispatched promptly. The individual who initiated the gift should have already discussed the certificate with the donor to explain the policy the institution follows in acknowledging the collection and forwarding the certificate. The collection can then be moved into the stack area, its location noted and schedules drawn up for its arrangement and description.

Archives which accession only the records of their own institution will not encounter many of the problems that manuscript repositories do. If the staff of the parent institution has been well-informed, the archival material should arrive at the archives in a relatively good order with a cover sheet indicating the type of records, outside dates, official transferring material, ultimate disposition of the material, a detailed list of the material by description of its significant series or subseries of records. However, in a great many institutions where the archival program is just beginning or where records management has not been possible, the archives will find itself in need of a definite and involved inventory process because some administrators, like many of the individuals involved with manuscript collections, have used horizontal pile techniques for filing systems or have removed material arbitrarily from their files.

Arrangement and Description

The arrangement and description of the collection and the development of a comprehensive finding aid are the critical procedures carried out to make collections usable. Unlike library work where individual units, such as books, are cataloged and entered into a card catalog individually, archivists and manuscript curators have to deal with a volume of material that cannot be described or indexed on an item-by-item basis except for the most extraordinarily valuable material. Archivists deal with records in a collective form.

The finding aid developed by most archives and the majority of manuscript repositories is the real key to the utilization of any particular collection and the finding aids serve collectively as the tool for utilizing the holdings of an entire repository. The finding aid is essentially a tool describing the various series and subseries that are really the organic parts of a group of records or

Overview

personal papers. During the development of the preliminary inventory, the staff member examining the papers should be enough aware and conversant with the records and papers to begin to identify the various units within the collection that have a functional organizational unity. Obviously, for manuscript collections that come in no order whatsoever, a great deal of intensive study and reflection must be undertaken to gain an understanding of the collection and to map out a systematic and logical arrangement.

Whether dealing with official government records or the personal papers of a local individual, the staff member responsible for the arrangement and description of the collection should seek progressively to describe the collection in greater detail. The preliminary inventory, if done well, may serve as a provisional finding aid; however, the final arrangement and description of the collection and the detailed finding aid developed will facilitate research use as well as staff management of the collection.

The main effort in arranging the material is to bring the papers that have a functional unity together if they are not already related, so that they can then be described in some collective measure. Most manuscript repositories that are dealing with anything less than an extremely large collection may want to include, either with the finding aid they publish or at least in the archive or manuscript files themselves, a detailed folder list to the collection to facilitate researcher use and staff control over the collection. The folder list can be developed as the individual staff member is going through the files, arranging the materials, substituting acid-free folders and reboxing the materials into acid-free archival boxes. While this work is routine and many times thought of as a less prestigious task in the manuscript or archival operation, it is certainly one of the more critical.

Some repositories have gone beyond trying to establish control at the folder level and have tried to generate a calendar which individually describes the physical characteristics of each item in the collection along with a brief narrative or abstract describing the intellectual content. The calendar, while helpful to the researcher, is extremely wasteful of staff time. It is not justified except for the most important material. Time spent on calendaring a collection might better be spent gaining better control of more collections, unless, of course, there is nothing better to do—an unusual situation in most archives or manuscript repositories.

Overview

Computers are being utilized in large institutions to develop comprehensive finding aids. Once the collection has been arranged and described, a computer printout of the finding aid or an index to the aid can be generated. The computer can manipulate the data to provide information on the collection by personal or corporate name, by subject, by folder order and so forth. The expertise and funds needed to implement an effective computer program are usually available only to the largest archival agencies. Without in-house computer programmers and analysts, dependable and relatively inexpensive access to a computer and a great amount of patience and determination, an attempt to utilize the computer to index collections is bound to be frustrating and disappointing.

Once the series descriptions and the folder index are completed, you may wish to consider a limited publication of the finding aid. In the case that you do, you may want to include a brief biographical sketch of the individual involved or brief corporate history and also a preface describing the collection very generally, how it arrived at the archives and how it relates to other materials in your archives or other repositories. If you have one or two important and outstanding collections the publication of a register is not only pleasing to the donor, obviously, but could be used as a tool to interest other prospects, indicating to them how materials are arranged and described and made available in your agency.

Unlike libraries, no attempt is made to file material by subject. Stack areas in archives and manuscript repositories are closed to all but staff members. Record groups and collections of papers are usually shelved in serial order as they are arranged, described and made available for research. No attempt is made to place similar material together. Closed stacks provide additional security and also allow the institution to utilize compact or high-density shelving to accomodate the maximum amount of material in the minimum amount of space.

Preservation

Any archives or manuscript repository, no matter what its size, has the responsibility to preserve the material entrusted to it as carefully and as skillfully as possible. While large institutions can employ staff members with a specialized knowledge of preservation problems, any archives should be able to take the beginning and basic steps to ensure the preservation of the treasures entrusted to it. Temperature control, humidity control, if possible, and an obsession for good clean housekeeping are three of the major emphases any repository should make. Perennial, sub-zero storage of records would slow down any chemical reaction or changes in the papers, but obviously a compromise has to be made in terms of staff comfort and searcher utilization of the materials. Temperatures between 68° and 70° and between 40 and 50 percent relative humidity seem to be the compromise acceptable to most institutions. It is important that the temperature and the humidity be relatively stable because fluctuating changes in these environmental conditions damage records.

Housekeeping is an important consideration, not only for the preservation of collections, but also for staff comfort, safety and morale. Some collections coming in to repositories will have been stored under incredibly poor conditions and will demand a great deal of staff time in cleaning, fumigating and other care before any substantial work can be done with them.

Many manuscript collections contain vast amounts of material on poor quality paper that is yellowing and disintegrating quickly. The use of acid-free file folders and boxes can help to mitigate acid migration and further deterioration of the paper, but more sophisticated techniques may be in order. Light, particularly fluorescent and daylight, accelerate degradation of papers as does urban air pollution. While some specialized techniques can be done by an enthusiastic, yet well-trained, staff, some very sophisticated techniques are best left to professionals who would provide services to you.

Users

One of the most rewarding aspects of being in a small operation is the opportunity to work with prospective donors, arrange for the transfer of material, have a hand in the processing of collections, and as a reward for those efforts, to see an intelligent, capable patron utilizing the material that you have gathered and cared for. The initial contact you and your staff have with the researcher is critical for setting the tone of the relationship. It is important that you convey the fact that you have a very valuable historical resource that has been carefully prepared and preserved. This,

Overview

coupled with helpful and courteous service, will do much to impress the patron with the job your agency is trying to do and the importance of being extremely careful with the material.

The researcher must be quickly oriented to the conditions of use of your collections, the conduct expected, and how your operations will respond to his needs. Staff members most familiar with the collection in the subjects he is interested in should be available for consultation and advice. As the patron indicates an interest in specific collections, finding aids should be provided along with any assistance the staff might give him. Any specific conditions of use or restrictions on the collection should be made clear immediately. The forms and material you use to orient patrons and to record their use of collections should also provide the data to make an analysis of the collections most heavily used, a count of the amount of use of the entire facility and information on other services that you provide. Such data can be utilized in defense of the budget which you have carefully thought out.

The introduction the repository gives to the researcher, the tone that is set and the physical arrangements for security should discourage or make impossible the theft of material or the accidental taking of these resources. While it might be almost impossible to deter a determined and unknown thief from taking material away, the arrangements you have made for registering users, supervision of the search room and visual inspection upon entering and leaving the room should discourage misuse of the collections.

Providing prompt, helpful service to patrons is certainly one of the joys of working in a small program. Much of the use may be by local amateur writers and historians seeking to gain further understanding of the community. Your conversations with these users should give you an insight into the history and developments of the subject field in which you are specializing in the collection of records.

No depository will attract users unless it makes its holdings known. News releases and photographs with cut lines forwarded to local news media not only indicate the progress you are making but also make prospective researchers aware of some of the holdings in your agency. Reports should also be made to the *National Union Catalog of Manuscript Collections* at the Library of Congress, using their data sheets, as well as reports to the American Historical Association and the Organization of American Historians, the Society of American Archivists, the Association of College and Research Libraries of A.L.A. and other interested professional groups. It is only by efforts of each repository to make the public aware of its holdings that researchers have any hope of knowing what materials are available, particularly those of more modern vintage. Timely announcement of acquisitions provides the only adequate justification for any archival program: use of the depository's holdings.

Good Sense and Good Judgment: Defining Collections and Collecting

Mary Lynn McCree

There is a small four-year women's college located in a middle western town of 50,000. Originally settled in 1830, the town is now the county seat of government. It is served by train, bus and interstate highways from a major metropolitan area located 50 miles away, containing several major colleges and universities. The private liberal arts college, founded in 1882, has an enrollment of 450 students, 80 percent of whom continue on to graduate school. In its almost 100 years of existence, it has counted among its graduates some famous and influential American women.

Quite suddenly and unexpectedly a member of the college's class of 1945 died. For the past 10 years she had served in the U.S. Congress, representing the district in which the college was located. She was also a member of the board of trustees of the college. Prior to being elected to Congress, she had been one of the first practicing women lawyers in the district, active in the civic affairs of the area, and an early proponent of women's rights. In her spare time she wrote poetry. One of her collections of poems won a Pulitzer prize.

During her lifetime she had accumulated a sizable personal archive. Her husband felt it should be preserved. After all, other congressional representatives preserved their papers by presenting them to an educational institution of their choice. He believed a fitting place for her papers would be her alma mater. Accordingly, he approached the president of the college offering, not only the congresswoman's archives, but a $20,000 scholarship fund in her name as well.

The college president knew her institution had no manuscript collection, yet primarily because of the scholarship proposal, she convinced herself that perhaps it should have one, and without hesitating, she accepted the gift, informing the college librarian of the new acquisition. The gift was made with the understanding that the college would add other appropriate collections to that of the congresswoman to create a prestigious and recognized manuscript repository.

Defining Collections

As soon as announcement of the gift was made in the local newspaper, the librarian began to receive calls from individuals offering a variety of material to add to the manuscript collection being organized at the college. Was the library interested in the family correspondence of a pioneer settler of the town? Would it be appropriate to present the archives of the local women's club? A professor inquired as to whether the college was going to gather its own archives, for she had some papers she felt should be deposited. Clearly, the librarian, or someone, had to come to terms with what kind of collection the college was going to create.

Establishing a Collecting Policy

The librarian was confronted with the same issue all other archivists and librarians face or should try to face when they initiate and create a collection of primary source materials to be used for scholarly inquiry and research. Too many institutions refuse to address the problem of adopting a collecting focus and their manuscript collections grow higgily-piggily, with little prestige or recognition from the scholarly world.

The librarian realized that the congresswoman's papers could provide the impetus to building a variety of manuscript collections, each with a different focus. After some consideration, the librarian singled out five separate ideas that she felt should be explored further for possible development as a collecting policy:

1　Papers of individuals and organizations revealing the growth and development of the town and county;

2　Papers of influential women and women's organizations in the town, county, state, or perhaps in the Middle West for a given time period;

3　Papers of political figures from an as yet undefined geographic area to include the town in a specific time period;

4　The papers and writings of literary figures of the state or the Middle West for a specific time period;

5　Development of the college's own archives.

Let us consider which of these topics is most appropriate for the college to adopt as its collecting policy. Almost all of these topics

Defining Collections

are defined by subject, geographic area and time period. While it is important to have some definition in any collecting policy that is developed, it is equally important to create a guideline with some flexibility so that the collection has some room to grow and evolve.

Many manuscript collections in America today were started, like the one at this midwestern women's college, because an individual or an organization presented its papers to a library, historical society, college or university. By accepting those papers, the institution signals its willingness and ability to assume responsibility for the maintenance of that gift for the benefit of the larger scholarly community. It also implies an intent to create a manuscript collection composed of the papers of individuals and organizations who have participated in or observed a series of activities relating to the focus that the institution has elected to establish.

In this regard, an institutional collection is far different from a collection of manuscripts and related items gathered by an individual. The private collector may select a person, event, or subject around which to build his collection, e.g., Franklin Delano Roosevelt, the American Civil War, American women novelists of the nineteenth century. He is interested in individual items for their uniqueness or autograph more than for their informational value. He is often content if he can boast complete "sets" of the autographs, for instance, the Northern generals who saw action during the American Civil War or a signed F. D. R. note or letter on letterhead stationery from each of the offices F. D. R. held. The private collector builds his collection almost entirely through purchase.

An institution, on the other hand, is not interested just in the unique item, but rather in complementary, interrelated bodies of consecutive files of manuscripts that provide detailed information on a person, event, organization, period of time or subject. These manuscripts when viewed together tell a story; the content of the documents is more important than the autograph value. This does not mean that institutions with manuscript collections would turn down unique and autographically valuable manuscripts. They wouldn't. But their primary responsibility is to create a focused body of materials that informs the scholar.

Does an institution know when it receives an initial gift what additional materials it should seek in order to develop a unified collection? Usually, no. Neither has it considered what such a commitment means in terms of personnel, facilities and money. The extent and focus of the collection have a direct bearing on the personnel, facilities and funding necessary to maintain it, and vice versa. Therefore, it seems logical that one of the first prerequisites for establishing a manuscript collection is defining a collecting policy. This should be done before any additional manuscript materials are added to the initial gift collection. How does the institution develops is collecting policy? What are some of the considerations?

Whether the manuscript collection begins with a gift collection or with nothing but an idea of what the institution might like to collect, a consideration of the course the development of a manuscript collection should take depends on an assessment of the following: the institution's resources, resources available for use from other area institutions, and the public the institution thinks it serves now and wants to attract in the future.

Manuscripts are not used in a vacuum. Scholars and students usually turn to primary resources only after they are familiar with the published works or secondary sources in their chosen field of inquiry. So, to begin with, survey your institution's scholarly resources to determine what secondary and other primary research tools it has that support the kind of manuscript collection you are considering. Look at your library's books, periodicals, newspapers, public documents, microfilm, record, tape and film collection, pamphlets, prints, maps, etc., to see if and how these holdings complement your intended collection focus. Then consider the resources available in other institutions in your immediate geographic area to discover if there are materials that would enhance and complement your projected manuscript collection. It usually makes very little sense to create a manuscript collection that has a focus completely alien to the interests of your institution and/or neighboring institutions, as expressed in secondary resources they have already gathered.

After you have assessed the depth of supporting resources, you will have some idea of how much material there is already on hand. If you discover there is little or no material of a secondary nature in close proximity, then you will have to consider either discarding the collecting focus you were considering or acquiring at least a basic bibliography of secondary resources as one of the costs of starting the collection.

Defining Collections

It is equally important to consider the economic consequences of creating a manuscript collection. Assess your institution's financial position, not only to determine if it can support the collection by acquiring or continuing to acquire secondary resources complementary to the collection, but also to ascertain whether it can provide the funds necessary to maintain staff to administer, process and service the collection, acquire the collection, and house it. Remember, it takes money to secure collections by purchase *or* by gift. If you believe that the necessary funding is available at present, ask yourself if it will be there in the future. Try to judge if there is a good possibility that the funding necessary to support a manuscript collection will be there in the increasing amounts required to maintain the initial collection or to build a growing collection.

For instance, a collection that you anticipate will be built largely through purchase will probably require more funding than one created through gifts. Yet if the collection you intend to build through gifts has a broad geographic focus, more funds will be required for identification of prospective collections, for deposit, travel and communications, than if you were creating a collection with a local focus.

Next, take a look at your staff. Manuscripts and archives are not processed into a collection or made available to the public in the same manner as printed library material. They require special handling by individuals trained in the theory and techniques of managing manuscript and archival resources. It is vital that you find and maintain well-qualified staff to support your collection, for it is worth little to the prestige of your institution, to students, scholars and researchers who wish to use it, if materials in the collection are inaccessible to them for lack of proper professional care.

Last, but certainly not least, you must consider the physical facilities required to maintain a manuscript collection. To begin with, there is simply a matter of having adequate space in which to store, process and service collections you anticipate receiving immediately. It should be a self-contained area to which you can limit access; it should be fireproof and waterproof. Controls to provide proper temperature, humidity and lighting are desirable.

But can your institution provide adequate long-term permanent space to process, house and service the manuscripts you anticipate receiving, given the collecting policy you are considering?

Defining Collections

How does the space your institution agrees to make available to you affect the kind of manuscript collection you can develop? If the space is small and there is absolutely no hope of enlarging the allotment you should be certain that the collection you plan can be contained in it. For example, you will probably require more space to preserve the papers of political figures and organizations which tend to create and maintain large correspondences than you would require for the manuscripts of a poet. Seeking and accepting papers when you have no means of preserving and protecting them is irresponsible and reflects discredit on your institution.

Once you have assessed these aspects—the supporting secondary and primary holdings, funding, personnel, physical facilities—of your institution's ability to maintain a collection, you should consider at least three other major issues: your institution's public, other institutions' collecting policies, and problems related to institutional archives.

When your institution commits itself to create and maintain a manuscript collection it is with the clear understanding that it is doing so for the benefit of the entire scholarly world. Your institution cannot in good conscience limit access to the collection it is creating to its own members, students or scholars. A manuscript collection should be open to qualified researchers who are willing to abide by the rules of use your institution establishes. So it becomes a matter of deciding which public you would most like to appeal to or to serve.

Usually, your first concern is to create a collection that will be useful to your most immediate constituency. A college or a university may wish to collect materials that will be useful to its own students or faculty, secondarily to the students and faculty of other institutions, free-lance writers and researchers, and amateurs. On the other hand an historical society might feel obliged to consider the interests of its membership, often times history buffs and leisure time scholars, as co-equal or more important than those of students and scholars. A collection with a local history flavor or focusing on some popular event, person or time will attract many more amateur scholars than the papers of less romantic, stellar subjects.

It is also important to remember that there are pitfalls in attempting to tailor a collection to the interests of one group of faculty or

Defining Collections

students, or one small pressure group. For example, there may be a faculty member doing research on the Japanese who have settled in your community since 1900. Though no one else has shown any interest in that topic and there are no secondary resources to support that interest, you accede to the faculty member's wishes and direct all your resources—staff time and funds—to collecting material for her. As soon as you begin to acquire some of the collections in which she is interested, she accepts a job offer on the West Coast. Faculty and students leave institutions, and pressure groups who are successful lose their *raison d'être* and fade to nothing. Then where is the public for whom you have developed your collection? It is your responsibility to create a collection that holds a continuing interest and relevance for scholars as a research and teaching tool. Hopefully, the manuscripts you select to preserve will be used over and over again for a variety of topics and points of view. Be sure that your public is broad enough to be continually supportive and interested.

Another major consideration in determining a collection development policy is knowledge of the established collecting policies of other institutions, particularly those in the area in which your institution is located. It would appear to be bad judgment to create and implement a manuscript collecting policy that duplicates one already functioning successfully within the geographic area that you propose to serve. Competition with an established, recognized collection is costly in terms of time, staff and funds. It leads to feelings of ill will between institutions. The scholarly world is better served and your own institution's reputation benefited by building a unique collection of resources formerly unavailable to scholarship. For instance, why should your institution collect local history materials if there is a historical society that already has an established collection consisting of papers that you have determined are central to a creditable collection. Strike off on a new direction, but try to be sure that what you are spending time, effort and money on has relevance for more than the immediate future, for more than a limited public.

It is wise for institutions to cooperate with one another, especially if they are located in the same geographic area. Be sure to know what other institutions are collecting so that should someone offer your institution papers which do not fall within the scope of your collection you might suggest another institution that would be a more appropriate home for the materials. For the same reason, communicate your collecting interests to other area institutions or appropriate repositories outside your locale. Perhaps they will send some collections your way.

A thorough knowledge of the collections of other institutions with collections development policies that overlap yours will save you the expense of pursuing a collection of papers already located in a repository. It will also help you provide better reference service to students and scholars using your collections, for you will be able to suggest other repositories near your institution which have materials that might be helpful.

A third major consideration is the existence of many institutional archives—archives of colleges, museums and the like—which preserve the documentation of their own institutions. Should you attempt to collect official records of other institutions which pertain to your subject area? The answer is "no" in virtually every case where an institutional archives is functioning effectively. What about the papers of individuals prominently associated with an organization which has an effective archives program? This is a more complex problem (the professor may be determined to destroy his papers before turning them over to his college), but those directing subject collections should not attempt to lure personal papers away from institutional archives. The pot of gold at the end of the rainbow—a complete archival subject collection- —is chimerical anyhow; important, unique segments of documentation in your subject area will always remain outside your grasp. Better techniques for achieving comprehensiveness are exchange of information about collections, and exchange of microfilm copies of closely related collections.

Now let us return to the problem faced by the librarian of the midwestern women's college. After considering the five prospective collection development policies in light of the foregoing criteria, she made her decision. The first possibility—developing a local history collection—was discarded when she discovered that the county historical society had been collecting local manuscript materials for the past 10 years. It had an established collection used mostly by genealogists and local history buffs, a clientele she had decided she did not wish to cater to. Likewise she discarded the third suggestion—collecting the papers of prominent political figures from her state—and the fourth—collecting the papers and manuscripts of leading literary figures from the Mid-

dle West. In both cases she discovered another institution with a
well established reputation for collections it had developed in
these two areas. The state historical society collected political
materials; one of the universities located in the nearby metropolitan area had been collecting the papers and manuscripts of midwestern literary figures for about 50 years.

That left two options: to focus on collecting the papers of women
and women's organizations in the Middle West or to establish a
college archive. A survey of her institution and those in the surrounding area revealed a sizable holding of secondary and primary resources on women and the woman's movement. She
knew that her own institution had some courses that stressed the
contributions women had made to life in the United States. She
also discovered that two universities in the large city had programs and courses at both the graduate and undergraduate levels
to explore the problems, experiences, and contributions of
American women. After a discussion with her institution's president, the librarian was reassured that adequate funds would be
available on a continuing basis to create a sizable and noteworthy
collection. The president seemed eager to gather and preserve a
unique collection of materials which might bring her institution to
national prominence, for the librarian had discovered only two
similar collections in existence in America—one on the East
Coast and one on the West. Both women reasoned that developing and preserving such a collection for the Middle West would
not only support the research and teaching needs of their own
institution but attract scholars, students, writers and journalists
from throughout the Midwest. It would appeal to the kind of public the institution wanted to support. The librarian and the president were convinced that this was the focus they should adopt for
their manuscript collection. But what of the college archives?
They decided to consider the development of the archives as a
facet of the broader collecting focus on women of the Midwest.
The college was an organization which for nearly 100 years had
educated influential women who made contributions in America.

Implementing the Policy

Now the institution had a collecting policy that it believed to be
feasible; one it hoped would make a contribution to scholarly
knowledge. How should it be implemented and how might that

action affect the collection scope? There are two major ways to acquire manuscripts, by purchase or by gift. Most collections are created by relying on both dealer and donor. These two individuals are instrumental in giving definition to a collecting policy.

Before you approach either of them it is necessary that your institution have considerable knowledge about the field it has chosen as a focus for its collection. Not only should the archivist or librarian activating the program be familiar with the major published secondary sources but also he or she should identify the individuals and organizations which have been signally involved in the events, movements and time periods with which the collection is concerned. It is imperative that an institution identify the resources it wishes to collect. The published interpretations of historians may help you make some of the judgments regarding records that should compose the collection; however, in many cases you will have to decide on the basis of your own knowledge of the subject, the papers you should seek. Do not hesitate to enlist the advice and help of scholars with special knowledge or experience doing research on subjects that fall within the scope of your collection.

Be sure you understand the type of documentation you are seeking in collections you acquire. Original and unique documents consisting of correspondence, diaries, memoranda, manuscripts of articles, books, speeches, notes, etc., are some of the types of documents that should compose most collections. Generally, do not concentrate on gathering numerous duplicates of published or copied items. Do not seek types of materials already part of a library collection, e.g., newspaper clippings, reprints and offprints of articles. Be familiar with the kind of materials that provide good meaty information that will make the papers you acquire so beneficial to scholars. Once you are certain that you have a good understanding of the information available on the subject matter of the collection, as well as an idea of the types of papers you want to acquire, you are ready to approach dealers and donors.

Dealers

An experienced manuscript dealer can be a tremendous help to an institution building a scholarly collection. Explain your collecting focus to the dealer. Let him know the kind of material you are looking for; let him know that you have funds from which you can draw to purchase appropriate items for your collection. The dealer's daily business includes his familiarization with all American autograph markets and many in other countries. If he knows what the boundaries of your collection are, he can become your eyes, not only prepared to note if, when and where an item or items are offered, but to track down *any* rumor that some particularly attractive morsel may come upon the market. Frequently, the dealer becomes the clearinghouse between seller and purchaser, receiving an agreed-upon commission on the successful transaction. He is also prepared to offer advice about appropriate items that you may not be aware of.

For all of these reasons, it is important that the dealer with whom you work is familiar with your growing collection. He is equipped and alert to channel items to particular customers, and this he normally does in a personal communication without waiting for the publication of his catalogs. He is customarily willing to submit material on approval if an institution well-known to him requests that it be mailed for inspection. The request is not made, it is generally understood, unless the institution is fairly certain that it wishes to purchase the offering. The material, if not bought, must be returned at once, since delay may result in the loss of its sale to someone else. The librarian is bound to observe fully the well-defined ethics of approval shipments (no copying of any kind; recognition that having an item temporarily in your possession does not allow you any rights to its contents.)

A dealer guarantees the authenticity of any item you purchase through him. If at any time the authenticity of an item can be authoritatively challenged, it may at once be returned to the dealer. Dealing with a reputable dealer is best protection from the risk of either being unmercifully taken by deliberately unscrupulous persons or purchasing either stolen material or facsimiles or forgeries. A dealer's reputation rests on his ability to guarantee his stock. Often, manuscripts you would like to own come up for sale on the auction market. Here a friendly dealer can be a help, too, for the dealer who frequently secures materials in the auction market is much more familiar with peculiarities of the market than the librarian. You will have a better chance of securing materials you want that are to be offered at auction if you engage a reliable and experienced dealer. This does not mean that the librarian should not be in attendance at the sale. Obviously, when the dealer is to represent an institution, the two should confer in advance to determine the maximum amount the latter is willing to pay. And always, if the dealer is able to buy below the maximum set, he will do so and save his customer.

No reputable dealer will ever represent two clients in bidding for the same item. It may occasionally happen that both a client and the dealer are interested in acquiring the same item. In such cases, if the client's declared maximum is higher than that of the dealer, the latter, accepting his client's bid, will not compete. And should he, representing his client, find it possible to obtain the item at less money than he himself would have paid, he would still turn over the item to his client. If, on the other hand, the dealer's intended bid exceeds that of the client, the client is expected to withdraw his bid, permitting the dealer to obtain it.

The dealer's fee, as the institution's representative, is customarily 10 percent of the sales price. He has earned this fee by guaranteeing the purchase's authenticity as a document and as the document described for sale by the auction house. He has also provided his expertise and experience with regard to current market values and the delicacies of buying at an auction. American auction houses now usually provide an approximate valuation of items to be sold in advance of their sale. Unfortunately, these estimates are often low—someone bidding the recommended fair market price often loses out on the item. Again, rely on an experienced dealer to give you a better idea of what the items you are interested in should cost. Dealers, when they buy at such sales, are permitted a limited period of credit, but other buyers are requested to pay at the time of purchase.

A word of caution, however. Remember, dealers are in business to sell manuscripts. You must be the ultimate judge of whether or not you can afford an item or whether it is what you need in the collection you are building. Know your collection, be honest and firm about your needs, pay your bills promptly, and you and the dealer with whom you work should have a long and respectful relationship.

Donors

While many institutions rely on dealers for individual specific items to highlight or fill in their collections, many try to acquire the bulk of their collections through gifts. Just as dealers help an institution develop a collecting policy, so do donors. Not only do they present their papers, which may provide important and hitherto unknown information, they also provide suggestions and leads to new prospective donors who usually have created collections which are complementary to theirs. So it is vital that you achieve a good continuing relationship with an individual or organization who places papers in your collection.

As with the dealer, honesty is always the best policy. Establish the credibility of your institution and your collection with a donor. Explain the scope of your collection, why his papers are important to it. Tell him the kinds of people who will seek access to his papers and the probable uses to which they will be put. If it is appropriate, provide information on copyright, literary rights and appraisal. Let him know that your institution accepts responsibility for the preservation of the papers it believes to be of value to scholars. If he is interested, explain some of the procedures of arrangement and description, some of the methods used to guarantee their safety, including physical facilities, that your institution provides.

A donor who respects you and your institution will willingly provide information on his own collection that will be helpful, not only as you prepare his papers for use by scholars, but also as you seek leads to other collections. He may even be willing to vouch for your collection personally to those other prospective donors, thus providing the person-to-person contact, usually a more persuasive method of establishing the donor relations than a phone call or a letter from an unknown source.

Conclusion

Establishing a collecting policy is a multifaceted activity. It requires knowledge of your institution and its public, of manuscript collections and how they operate, and of the subject you select as the focus for your collection. After you have the collections development policy you feel you can live with, write it down, abide by it as you go about creating a manuscript collection, and review it frequently. Good luck!

Arrangement and Description of Manuscripts

Richard C. Berner

Before attempting arrangement of any accession, certain basic archival concepts should be clearly understood. These are: the principle of provenance, the integrity of the papers/records,[1] and original order.

Provenance relates to the origins of the papers, the activity which generated them. They are one form of documentary remains left by human activity. Consequently they will reflect those actions in documentary form. It is because human activity occurs in a socio-historical context that the configuration itself will be most faithfully reflected by keeping the papers together according to the source that created them in the first place. Out of recognition of this fact, the principle of provenance has been developed; it is the basic premise of archival theory and practice. All else has been developed from it. Flowing directly from this principle is concern for the integrity of the papers, *respect des fonds.* By respecting their integrity, the librarian's temptation to classify elements in the accession by subject or other device will be avoided. Manuscript accessions do not conform to the characteristics of publications and are not amenable to subject classification. Unlike the defined subject of a publication, subject matter in manuscript sources is diffuse, varying from item to item and within an item itself.

In addition, human activity occurs serially, in relation to events and developments. If the integrity of the papers is respected, this activity, occurring over time and in relation to other social action, will be more faithfully reflected. When it is in turn related to other manuscript and archival documentation in the repository itself and elsewhere, it is possible to show interrelationships which would be made more difficult if integrity of the papers were not observed.

The user of manuscript and archival sources cannot be expected to discover the contents of a manuscript collection by hunch and accident. On the contrary, the archivist must reveal those contents by techniques of arrangement and description so that the researcher can make maximum use of those resources. Since 1961 he has even been able to use a national network which relates resources of hundreds of manuscript collections to one another nationwide in the form of the *National Union Catalog of Manuscript Collections.*

The Hierarchy of Arrangement and Control

Before continuing the discussion of arrangement and description at this point, it is well to become acquainted with the five different record levels: the record group, subgroup, series, file folder and items levels.[2] It does not matter that these concepts are derived from archival theory and practice, and not from that of librarianship. The items to be dealt with in manuscript collections, most of which are housed in libraries, are not different from the items which appear in archives. Most manuscript repositories contain archives of private origin, personal as well as corporate. In recent years the management of manuscript collections has responded to recognition of this common feature. Consequently, archival theory and practice are now being generally applied to the management of manuscript collections.

The hierarchy of controls, noted above, concerns both arrangement and description. By implication and in practice this hierarchical concept can also become the basis for a system that establishes processing priorities within the repository. For example, if there is no current demand for access to a particular acquisition at the time it is received and if none is anticipated in the near future, then control can be accepted at the record group and subgroup levels. The intent should be geared to meeting existing and anticipated user needs by providing better access to the most important accessions and to those in current demand.

In addition, it is well to bear in mind that many accessions tend to be self-accessing by reason of being the product of organized activity. To the extent that the files have been kept orderly by the person or corporate body they will be self-accessing just as they were while being used in relation to the activity they now serve to document. The archivist, in trying to perfect an original order or by establishing an orderly arrangement, is, in addition, making the files self-accessing. In the section below on subject access there will be a more extended discussion of how techniques of arrangement and description can aid scholarly access to archives.

Formats for Finding Aids

It should be clear from the introduction that archives and manuscript collections differ markedly from publications. Some of these differences will become more apparent in what follows. In the matter of description, it is quickly evident. All description for a given collection can fall under the general heading of "Finding Aids." Historically two basic forms of finding aids have developed. The card catalog understandably developed first because most manuscript collections were administered by librarians. Gradually the page format was introduced to compensate for the deficiencies of the card format. Consequently most repositories now employ two kinds of finding aids:

1   A page form of description for selected accessions in the form of a register like that of the Library of Congress[3] or a variant of the "preliminary inventories" of the National Archives.

2   Catalog entries in card form for each accession. It is the card catalog that gives access to the entire manuscript collection. Entries in it serve as a partial index to those accessions which are also described in page format. Few repositories use only the page format exclusively (one for each accession) while fewer still have developed cumulative name, subject and chronological indexes to each of their "inventories."[4]

Usually there are entries in the card catalog for each accession. In addition a description in page format will often be made for selected accessions, depending often on their size and importance. As a general rule, it is good practice to make a form of preliminary inventory, like a container listing, at the time of accessioning, following it with catalog entries. It should be recognized in this context that the catalog serves really as an index to the inventories. It is the page form of finding aid that is cataloged, not the "manuscripts." As such the entries can contain merely the slightest amount of information, such as those in typical book indexes or as much as appears on catalog cards appearing in the NUCMC format.[5] The librarian should judge how much detail is needed on the catalog card to lead the user to the material. For accessions for which there are both a page form of description

Arrangement and Description

and catalog card entries, the latter will lead the user to the former and from there to more precise locations in the accession itself. If this can be accomplished with few words, the card will be more effective.

Although the traditional card catalog is a form of indexing employed at most manuscript repositories, a simpler form like that used within books is also possible. It is also considerably less expensive and can be more comprehensive. At the national level such an index is used for the *National Union Catalog of Manuscript Collections.* Its volume indexes are not at present cumulated into one sequence. Proper and place names and topics are in one alphabetical sequence. It has no chronological index. With some modification it can serve as a model for indexing at the repository level where somewhat different emphases are needed and where a different view of bibliographical control can be developed.

For example, if control of proper names is the major route to subject access, and the subject headings which are used apply mainly to the primary subject content of the accession as a whole (not to the variable subject matter within individual file units and items), then it may be wise to separate the cumulative subject index from that for proper and place names. Also, a separate cumulative chronological index is usually desirable at the repository level.

Achieving Initial Control: The Group or Accession

With this initial discussion of the character of archives and the consequent nature of the means of control of archives as background, a description of practical steps to be taken can begin.

When papers are received one of the first steps is to determine their order, recognizing that probably there will be a difference between the received order at the time of accessioning, and the original filing arrangement of the papers. If the papers are in their original filing arrangement upon arrival, then the task of arrangement is simplest, there being no larger task than transferring the materials to acid-free folders in their existing order. Usually, however, some rearrangement of the received order is needed to reestablish the original filing system. It is important to note that serialism is the basis of "order," just as it is of activity.

Arrangement and Description

With this in mind the arranger can invent a filing system if none is apparent or if only a partial one is discernible.

Once this first step is completed, and assuming for illustration that nothing is done to alter the received order of the papers, a description could be done which would reflect only the primary characteristics of the accession as a whole. This description would represent bibliographical control at the record group level. This can be done in the following manner. Normally some subject characteristics will have been expected inasmuch as negotiations for the papers would have originated for that very reason. By examining the papers, however briefly, such expectations can be quickly confirmed or quashed. If the latter, there may be reason to return the accession to the donor unless there are other redeeming qualities. In either case, the primary subject characteristics can be learned quickly and appropriate subject entries can be made immediately in the card catalog or indexes.

In addition, by scanning file folder headings in the correspondence series or by leafing through unarranged papers it is often possible to note the names of major correspondents; enter them also in the card catalog or indexes. By making such entries, access to the papers is made possible from the time of accessioning. The user will know at least that somewhere in that accession will be documentation relating to the subject for which there was a subject entry, or some item(s) written by someone for which there was an author entry. The reference will lack precision but the user will be in the pasture where there is forage.

Often it is possible to actually make a summary inventory or container listing prior to doing any major rearrangement of the papers. This can be done by simply numbering the containers serially and listing the file folder headings in the order they appear. The result would be control at the record group level along with random control at the file folder level, but without arrangement of folders into subgroups and series.

Achieving Further Control: The Subgroup

Another way of achieving a better level of control at the time of accessioning is to establish subgroups for each of the separate corporate activities represented in the accession. This can frequently be done with minimal effort. The result is to gain control at the subgroup level. If this were to be followed by a container listing, there would again be partial control to the file folder level even if the folders have not yet been arranged into record series within the subgroup. (The role of the container listing in the over- all description will be indicated below.)

Example 1

UNIVERSITY OF WASHINGTON
Archives and Manuscripts Division

WORK SHEET

1. Accession no.   2. Name of Accession

   3149   **BAKER, Elizabeth, 1915-**

3. Date received **5/3/72**   4. Location

5. Donor or source **Ms. Baker**   Address: **Seattle**

                                         City   State

6. Biographical/historical features, and primary activity documented
Public official, civic ldr. Seattle City Councilwoman 1952-68. Active, League of Women Voters, Ld, Wash. Equal Rts. Amendmt Campaign. Born Seattle 1915 of pioneer Wash. family.

7. Types of record series **Family records to ca. 1860, corresp. + supporting papers re her various activities.**

8. Inclusive dates of records   Quantity **15 cartons**
ca 1860-1972

9. Names of major correspondents (use continuation sheet if needed)
   Democratic Party
   Clinton, Gordon S.
   Mitchell, Hugh B.
   Rosellini, Albert   **see continuation sheet**

10. Names of subgroups (use continuation sheet if needed)
   Seattle. City Council   **Equal Rts. Amendment Comm.**
   League of Women Voters. Seattle

11. Subjects. Topics: **Pol & govt. - Wash - Seattle**
                  " " - women
         Names: **League of Women Voters, Seattle**
                 Seattle. City Council
                 Equal Rts. Amendment Committee

12. Filing plan (use reverse side if necessary)
   ① **1st subgroup acc/to different corp. functions**
   ② **re Family papers review with curator before arranging**
   ③ **After subgrouping review with curator before arranging into series.**

Arrangement and Description

Example 2a

1. Name of accession Baker, Elizabeth, 1915 -

2. Type of material Family papers, correspondence and supporting

   files, ca. 1860-1972

3. Location BIIIB 4/1-7

4. Size 15 cartons

5. Source Mrs. Elizabeth Baker (Albert) 3 May 1972,   #3149

6. Biographical / historical features
   Politician, civic leader
   Born 1915, married, Stanley Albert, 1943
   Active, League of Women Voters
   Head, Washington State Equal Rights Amendment Committee
   Seattle City Councilwoman, 1952-1968
   Active, Democratic Party

7. Names of major correspondents / names

   Democratic Party
   Clinton, Gordon S.
   Rosellini, Albert
   Mitchell, Hugh B.
   Magnuson, Warren G.
   Adams, Brockman

   See continuation sheet

8. Special restrictions: Scholarly research

9. Literary property rights: Dedicated to public

10. Subjects covered:
    Topics   Names
    Politics & government - Wn - Seattle

                                              League of Women Voters. Seattle
    Politics & government - women   Seattle. City Council
                                              Equal Rights Amendment Committee

Example 2b

```
Baker, Elizabeth, 1915 -
    Papers, ca. 1860 - 1972
    City Councilwoman of Seattle, active in League
of Women Voters and Democratic Party, Chairwoman
State Equal Rights Amendment Campaign, family papers.
Includes correspondence, reports, ephemera, related
materials.  Major correspondents...

Consult guide/inventory for more detail.

[Subject tracings]
```

By routinely doing this kind of work at the time of accessioning the repository will have structured a comprehensive control over the entire manuscript collection. From such a base it is then possible to establish priorities in the processing program for the manuscript collection as a whole, deciding which accessions should receive first attention in getting in-depth controls.

To see how this procedure for establishing controls can be routinized see the work sheet (Example 1). A work sheet or accession register should be filled out for each accession upon its receipt. Note that on the bottom of the work sheet processing instructions are indicated. Once all of the information on the work sheet, except processing instructions, is transferred to catalog cards or to a basic data sheet (Examples 2a, 2b), the work sheet may be filed in a processing file, inasmuch as only processing information remains unconverted to a different format in finalized form. The accession register is a formal record, containing the same kind of information, but usually it will be filed by donor's name or number.[6]

In more explicit terms, what does control at the subgroup level mean? Accessions to modern manuscript collections usually contain several hundred items; typically their size is measured in linear feet. Virtually all such accessions will have record series characteristics. Some will also have record subgroup characteristics. Procedurally, before seeking series identification, an attempt should be made to identify subgroups. Normally there will be foreknowledge indicating whether or not a person whose papers have just been received has been involved in corporate activities that are separate from his/her directly personal affairs. In modern manuscript collecting it is typically these various corporate activities which supply the main motive for seeking that person's papers. From this knowledge of a person's career, the arranger of the papers will know what to look for as the basis of subgrouping.

Levels of Control Illustrated

In order to understand the successive stages through which control can proceed, the processing and description of a single accession will be followed, illustrating control at the subgroup level, at the series level, and at the file folder level. Note that focus is upon the container listing, inasmuch as levels of control appear in it, not elsewhere in the description. The elements which comprise the overall description include:

Name of the accession
Provenance (source of accession and how the papers were
   generated)
Biographical or historical highlights
Main record types
Size or volume of accession
Inclusive dates of papers
Table of contents, if appropriate
Mention of any unusual characteristics of the papers
Container listing
Index of names
Subject index

Statement of Example

Elizabeth Baker has given her personal and family papers to the manuscript collection. She was born in 1915 of a pioneer family, her grandfather having migrated to Washington Territory in 1862 and her grandmother in 1870. She married Stanley Albert in 1943, but has retained her maiden name. Ms. Baker became active in precinct committee work in the Democratic Party in King County in the late 1930s. She became active in the League of Women Voters in the 1940s (later its president), and in 1952 was elected to the Seattle City Council, serving until 1968. In 1971 she served as Chairwoman of the Washington State Equal Rights Amendment campaign.

Subgroup Level of Control Illustrated

To establish control at the subgroup level Elizabeth Baker's papers were arranged into identifiable subgroups, as noted in the example. Subgrouping is done by grouping folders and items

Arrangement and Description

according to the various separate corporate activities in which the person engaged. Those which could not be placed in a subgroup at the preliminary stage have been temporarily designated as personal papers. The container listing follows:

Box No.

1, 2	**Democratic Party**	1936-70
	Correspondence, campaign literature, scrapbooks, photographs, committee records.	
3-5	**League of Women Voters**	1944-51
	Correspondence, reports, publications, committee records, subject files.	
6-15	**Seattle. City Council**	1952-68
	Correspondence, committee records, subject files, campaign records, speeches, scrapbooks, clippings.	
16, 17	**Equal Rights Amendment Committee. Seattle**	1971-72
	Correspondence, reports, campaign literature, minutes of meetings, of Seattle ERA office.	
18	**Personal Papers**	c. 1930-60
	Correspondence, diary, miscellaneous writings, photographs.	
14, 15	**Family Papers**[7]	
	William Baker (grandfather)	c. 1860-1900
	Correspondence, diary, miscellaneous.	
	Liza Ames Baker (grandmother)	c. 1860-1920
	Some Ames family letters, diaries, photographs.	

From the listing above it is clear that there is little control beyond the subgroup level. But within each subgroup, it is possible to select names of some major correspondents, even at this preliminary stage. Options like this should be exercised when possible. Such names could then be noted as added entries on catalog cards or in a cumulative name index, in addition to making appropriate entries for each of the subgroups. The user would, by these means, be lead to the subgroup within which there are relevant items despite the fact that their precise location has not been established by the objective finding aids.

Catalog card entries for the Elizabeth Baker Papers controlled to the subgroup level could be made in the following manner:

```
              Baker, Elizabeth, 1915 -
                 Papers, 1860-72.  20 ft.
                    Correspondence, reports, committee re-
                 cords, ephemera, clippings relating to
Unit card        Seattle office of Equal Rights Amendment
                 Campaign, 1971-72, and to her work in
                 Seattle League of Women Voters, . . .


              (card 1 of 3)
```

Arrangement and Description

Name added entry (for subgroup)

```
League of Women Voters.   Seattle
Baker, Elizabeth, 1915 -
Papers, 1860-72.   20 ft.
     Correspondence, reports, committee records,
ephemera, clippings relating to Seattle Office
of Equal Rights Amendment Campaign, 1971-72,
and to her work in Seattle League of Women
Voters, . . .
```

Subject added entries can be made in standard style.

Series Level Control Illustrated

To illustrate control at the series level, one subgroup will be expanded, that for *Seattle. City Council.* Preceding the task of description, the papers would have been arranged into records series according to type of record, unless there is a recognizable original order which can be wholly or partially restored. It is assumed also that no refinement beyond grouping into series has been attempted; however, some general characteristics of each series are noted. A further assumption is that the size of the containers used at this stage are the same as in the subgrouping stage (10 x 12 x 15 cartons). At the next stage (file folder level) smaller acid-free containers will be used, requiring renumbering.

Box #		Approx. Items	Incl. Dates
6, 7	**Seattle. City Council**		
	General Correspondence. (With city, state, federal agencies, general public. Some major correspondents: Mayor's Office, Seattle Engineering, Lighting and Transit Departments, U. S. Federal Power Commission, Federal Housing Authority, Corps of Engineers, Washington State Public Utilities Commission, Legislative Council, Warren G. Magnuson, Henry M. Jackson, Thomas M. Pelly, Brockman Adams.) *See also* subject series and committee records for other general correspondence.	2.5'	1962-68
	Committee Records		
	Utilities Committee.	2.5'	1952-68
8, 9	*Skagit Project.* Correspondence with city, state, federal agencies, Canadian and British Columbia government agencies, International Joint Commission; hearings, reports.		
9	*California Intertie.* Correspondence with city, state, federal agencies; hearings, reports.	1'	1960-65

Arrangement and Description

10, 11	*Transit Committee*		1960-68
	Rapid Transit. Correspondence with city, state, federal agencies, citizen groups; hearings, reports *re* development of a rapid transit system for Seattle.	1′	1960-68
	Interstate-90. Correspondence with city, state, federal agencies, citizen groups; hearings, reports *re* development of rapid transit for greater Seattle intertie with I-90, Lake Washington Bridge.	1′	1966-68

From this description in page format, entries can be made in the card catalog. Although there are almost as many variations for form of entries as there are repositories, the following may be used. Refer to the NUCMC example in note 5 and notice the awkwardness of establishing series level control for that at any more refined level if the informational format is followed literally. However, by omitting the scope and contents note it is possible to include series information on one card. In the NUCMC example, the correspondence series in the King County Public Utility District Association subgroup could be noted:

```
King County Public Utility District Association
Spear, Lillian Sylten, 1897-1963.
   Papers, 1936-63.  7 ft. (ca. 6000 items)
   Correspondence, 1939-41, box 1, folders 1-15.*
```

In the case of the Seattle City Council subgroup of Elizabeth Baker's papers, the following series of card entries can be made for subgroup and series level control.

**Subgroup
Control**
```
Seattle.  City Council.  Utilities Committee.
Baker, Elizabeth, 1915 -
   Papers, 1860-1972.  20 ft.
   Seattle.  City Council.  Utilities Committee
   subgroup.  1952-68, in boxes 8 and 9.
```

---

*Interpretation: In the KCPUDA subgroup of Lillian Spear's papers, the correspondence series is in box 1, folders 1-15, for the years 1939-41.

Arrangement and Description

Series	International Joint Commission
Control	Baker, Elizabeth, 1915–
Within	Papers, 1860–1972. 20 ft.
Subgroup	Correspondence with IJC, 1952–68, box 8.*

If more detail is deemed necessary the last element can be:

Correspondence with IJC in Seattle City Council Utilities Committee subgroup *re* Skagit Dam Project, 1952-68, box 8.

As an alternative to the above form of card entry the same line of reference can be made more briefly by a simple index entry in page format.

International Joint Commission**

For manuscripts of the above, see Guides to the following collections:

Baker, Elizabeth papers 1860-1972		
Seattle. Lighting Department. Records 1905-63		
Puget Sound Power and Light Company. Records 1895-1960		

The decisions as to whether the card entry in its variant forms or a simple index entry is better depends upon how much information needs to be given at the initial point of reference. This is a policy decision, of course, but one which many, if not most, repositories do not realize can be made.

---

*Interpretation: In the Seattle City Council subgroup of Elizabeth Baker's papers, correspondence with IJC for 1952-68 will be found in box 8 of her papers.
**Interpretation: There will be items authored by the IJC not only in the papers of Elizabeth Baker which span the period 1860-1972, but also in the records of the Seattle Lighting Department and those of Puget Sound Power and Light Company. From these simple index entries the user would proceed to the container listing for each of these accessions for the more precise location and other information.

Arrangement and Description

Folder Level Control Illustrated

Assuming that internal processing priorities allow for establishing a more refined level of control over the papers of Elizabeth Baker, it has been decided to arrange each series into smaller file folder units, a finalized order. The following steps are entailed:

1 Establishing the final sequence of each item within each series.

2 Labeling each folder.

3 Placement into acid-free folders in units small enough for quick accessing, with care for physical condition of the items. Normally the first score mark (about ¼").

4 Placement of folders into acid-free containers.

5 Numbering each folder either in a single sequence or by using a box number prefix and beginning the folder number afresh for a box (5-1, meaning *box 5, folder 1).*

6 Listing file folder headings in each container.

7 Either making new catalog cards for the new listing, and withdrawing all previous ones, amending or replacing them, *or* making additional index entries in the cumulative indexes and correcting previous errors.

Expanding upon the example from the Elizabeth Baker Papers, let us assume that her correspondence with the International Joint Commission in relation to her Council Utilities Commission work has been placed in box 25, folders 13-15, of the new sequence. The new container listing will appear as follows:

Box/Folder		# of Items	Incl. Dates
	Committee Records		
	Utilities Committee		
	Skagit Project		
	Correspondence (alpha by correspondent)		
25/ 1-2	British Columbia. Economic Development Department	30	1952-68
3	Canada. Energy Council	13	1958-68
4	Canada. State Department	10	1965-68
etc.			
13-15	International Joint Commission	63	1952-68

From the above listing the precise folder number is referred to, providing control at the file folder level.

A catalog card entry could be made as follows:

```
International Joint Commission
Baker, Elizabeth, 1915 -
  Papers, 1860-1972.  20 ft.
  Correspondence with IJC, 1952-68, 63 items,
  box 25 folders 13-15.
```

As for the index entry for the IJC, if it is used instead of the card entry, no change is required because it already refers the user to the page format of description where more precise location information is provided.

The differences from the previous entry for series level control are that the number of items and the folder numbers are noted, the latter giving direct access to the folder(s) needed.

For the purpose of illustration, it was not indicated above that folders could have been numbered at the time of accessioning and a degree of control could have been attained at the file folder level. However, by proceeding as we have, it has been more clearly shown that stages of refining the arrangement go hand-in-hand with the precision of description. Furthermore, a sense of priorities has been conveyed with respect to the successive stages in refinement of arrangement and description.

No attempt will be made here to illustrate arrangement and description at the item level. As a general rule most repositories having voluminous twentieth-century accessions make little effort to attain item control. The reader should refer to the *Anglo-American Cataloging Rules* for guidance.

Special Arrangement Problems

The various types of correspondence—general and interoffice correspondence, incoming and outgoing letters, etc.—constitute the crucial record series in most accessions. It is through these series that name access is keyed, and subject access is heavily dependent upon bibliographical control of proper names.

For accessions in which correspondence items are without arrangement, in which incoming letters have been separated from

Arrangement and Description

their related response (outgoing letters), a high degree of name and chronological control can be achieved by establishing separate incoming and outgoing letters series. Incoming can be arranged alphabetically by name of correspondent, outgoing, chronologically, thereby providing two-way access, establishing an objective control over proper names.[8]

Outgoing letters are best arranged chronologically, if they have not previously been arranged in a different manner. In this way the sequential unfolding of events is most readily apparent. General correspondence includes both incoming and outgoing, interfiled and/or coupled. In the original order, general correspondence may be found in various arrangements: alphabetical by name of correspondent, in subject and case files, in a numerical system or whatever. Often as files become inactive they have been moved to make room for active ones; this leads to broken time series for any correspondent and constitutes a simple problem of rearrangement-by-consolidation for the manuscript repository. In those cases in which the arrangement is alphabetical, name control poses no problems. In other cases, it does. To deal effectively with this, the names of major correspondents within each file unit may be noted in the container listing and then entered as an added entry in the card catalog or in the cumulative name index, whichever is used. Example (using the above format):

Box
2-1   **California Intertie.** Correspondence with *Bonneville Power Administration, Columbia River Compact Commission, Federal Power Commission,* . . . Milton C. Mapes, . . . *Pacific Gas and Electric*

Note that all names italicized are in effect flagged for added entries.

While this method is more subjective than that in which incoming letters are filed alphabetically, it is much more objective than the kind of item selection (for entry) which was once a general practice and is becoming obsolete.

Subject files constitute a second special arrangement problem. Avoid creating subject files if they do not already exist. For existing subject files, it is normally best to leave them intact but to rearrange them within the original classification if the volume is unwieldy. By accepting the subject divisions created by the party who is the source of the files, there is the added advantage gained of more precise subject control and clues to the subject interests of the creator. Normally, in such file folders there will be a mixture of correspondence, clippings, reports, a range of diverse items

which for simplicity of access can be grouped into subseries.
Case and client files can be handled similarly. In effect, file units
of subject series are treated in the same manner as subgroups.
The difference is that subgroups represent separate corporate
activities, while subject series do not.

Enclosures must be handled very carefully in arrangement actions. Letters are a common form of enclosure. As a general rule if
it is attached to an incoming letter, keep it with that letter. However, if the letter is judged to be an enclosure but has become
separated from its covering letter, and if the sender cannot be
definitely determined, the letter should be filed by the name of the
addressee or writer, depending on the logic in the particular case.

Those letter enclosures which are copies should be retained with
their covering letters. Other types of enclosures include almost
anything, but typically they will be pamphlets, reports, clippings,
broadsides. Nonbulky items may be stapled to the verso of the
left-hand corner of incoming letters, or merely retained in the
same folder with the letter and any annotations that seem appropriate. It is advisable to enclose the item in folded bond paper if it
is likely to harm the covering letter by its high acid content.
Printed material of a more bulky character, such as pamphlets,
might best be separated from the correspondence series and
placed in a series for ephemera. Some notation in square brack-
ets might be made as cross-reference if the item is to remain with
the manuscript accession.

Nonmanuscript items are the last special arrangement problem
discussed here. Although this problem is dealt with in detail in
"Disposition of Nonmanuscript Items Found Among Manuscripts,"[9] some general guidelines can be indicated.

First, any nonmanuscript item which has been annotated should
be considered for retention with the accession because the anno-
tation has as much unique value as any other manuscript item.
For example, the books of Dylan Thomas which Theodore
·Roethke heavily annotated have been kept with the Roethke papers. In those cases in which the item is not in the library's collection of cataloged publications, an entry could be in the public
catalog, referring the user to the manuscript collection.

Items which are not annotated pose different problems. Ephemera are among the most common. Unless there is a unit in the

library established to handle ephemera, an ephemera series in the accession should be formed. If transferred elsewhere in the library, the rule of provenance should be applied by the receiving unit if at all feasible. Other nonmanuscript items should be handled in much the same way so that the user can be led easily and directly to all materials in the original accession wherever they might be. Expendable items, such as unmarked copies of books, government documents, journals, newspapers, and the like, should be sent to the appropriate library unit. As a general rule, it is good practice to list in some form all materials sent elsewhere. A further precaution is to require return of any items rejected by any receiving unit, so that item(s) can be considered for reincorporation into the original accession.

Proper Name Control and Subject Access

Probably the most direct access to the subject content of any accession is by the user's association of the name of a person or corporate body with the subject of his interest. Perhaps as much as 90 percent of user questions for access to manuscript collections is by this linkage of proper names to subject. What this clearly suggests is that the manuscript repository should concentrate upon getting a high degree of name control if it is to maximize subject access. The alternative is to go in the direction of a subject analysis of series, file folder units and individual items, which is expensive and unreliable because of the more highly subjective judgments that must be made. Subject analysis normally should be at the record group level, but may descend to the subgroup when some subgroup files do not share the primary subject characteristics of the accession as a whole. Descent to the series level also is justified for subject series (see below) on the same basis. For example, in the Council of Churches records, one subseries in its general subject series is *Japanese-American Evacuation and Relocation.* None of the subject headings used to characterize the primary subject contents of the accession would lead the user to this subject subseries; consequently one could be added to the subject headings for this accession. However, it should be noted that normally any reasonably knowledgeable user would have known already that the Council of Churches had been active on behalf of Japanese-American evacuees and this name association with this special subject would really be sufficient even without a special subject heading in the card catalog or cumulative subject index. These options should be carefully considered in developing modes of subject access.

Author Entry for Correspondence

As a general rule it is best to avoid a content analysis of a letter in determining the capacity in which the signer of a letter is acting. Normally it is sufficient to accept on its face that a person is acting in whatever capacity he/she signs, "Chairperson," "Councilman," "Mayor," "President, Mayors' Association of United States," etc. Ambiguities will occur, particularly for those who conduct a number of different corporate activities from the same office and where the form signature does not correlate with the content of individual letters. In a moderately large accession these idiosyncrasies will become evident during the course of processing the papers. Keywords in the text must be sought in such cases. Also these idiosyncrasies might be noted in the introductory section dealing with provenance ("how the files were created").

Furthermore, when it is clear that filing decisions are arbitrary, the user must be directed to look in more than one place for related or overlapping material. For example, John Brown (pseudonym) conducted a number of separate corporate activities while in the employment of one office (primary employer). Because his signature rarely indicated in what capacity he was writing, keywords in text were sought and used as a basis for sub-subgrouping within the overall subgroup—the name of his primary employer. Some could not be accurately classed by even this relatively intensive effort; these were left with the files of the primary employer. However, by keeping the sub-subgroups together with the files of the primary employer-subgroup, their interrelationships are also kept intact.

The National Union Catalog of Manuscript Collections

The main purpose in collecting manuscripts and archives is to make them available for research. Until 1961, when the first volume of the NUCMC was published, there had been no continuing effort to report accessions in a medium that was accessible nationwide. The NUCMC does this. It is therefore necessary that each repository accept a responsibility for reporting its accessions at a stage in the processing that will permit basic information to be reported accurately. This may be done on a NUCMC data sheet which should be sent upon completion to the Library of Congress for incorporation into the NUCMC. Because the information which is usable by the NUCMC need not be based on as precise bibliographic data as an accession that has been fully processed, it is possible to provide sufficient information at the series level of control, at which stage most of the major correspondents and subgroups will have been identified. By doing this, the accession is made accessible at the national and international levels quickly.

Notes

1 For simplicity the term *papers* or *records* individually will be used throughout, substituting for *papers/records.* The choice of one or the other will depend on the context of the discussion. Usage associates *papers* with personal files; *records* with files of corporate origin.

2 See Oliver Wendell Holmes, Jr., "Archival Arrangement—Five Different Operations at Five Different Levels," *American Archivist* 27 (no. 1, January 1964): 21-41.

3 Katherine E. Brand, "The Place of the Register in the Manuscripts Division of the Library of Congress," *American Archivist* 18 (no. 1, January 1955): 59-67.

4 For an extended analysis, see Richard C. Berner, "Manuscript Catalogs and Other Finding Aids: What Are Their Relationships?" *American Archivist* 34 (no. 4, October 1971): 367-372. See also Berner and M. Gary Bettis, "Description of Manuscript Collections; A Single Network System," *College & Research Libraries* 30 (no. 5, September 1969): 405-416.

5 Rules for cataloging according to NUCMC standards are in the *Anglo-American Cataloging Rules* (Chicago: American Library Association, 1967), Ch. 10. The unit card does not lend itself to series and finer levels of control, as will be shown.

```
Spear, Lillian Sylten, 1897-1963
    Papers, 1936-63.  7 ft. (ca. 6000 items)
    In University of Washington Library (Seattle)
    Teacher and civic leader.  Correspondence, minutes
of meetings, campaign material, and other papers re-
lating to the following organizations of which Mrs.
Spear was an official or secretary:  King County Pub-
lic Utility District Association, Public Ownership
League of Washington, Puget Sound Utility Commission-
ers' Association, Snohomish County
```

(continued on next card) MS 65-1055

6 Cf. Ruth Bordin and Robert Warner, *The Modern Manuscript Library* (New York: Scarecrow Press, 1966), pp. 35-36.

7 For convenience here, the collection of papers of her ancestors is treated as a corporate subgroup although they do not reflect her activity in any other capacity than that of Ms. Baker as a *collector*. Bearing this in mind, the family papers could be treated more directly as a separate accession under *Elizabeth Baker. Collector* or as *Baker Family Papers*.

8 For full rationale for this method, see Berner, "The Arrangement and Description of Manuscripts," *American Archivist* 23 (no. 4, October 1960): 395-406.

9 Richard C. Berner and M. Gary Bettis, "Disposition of Nonmanuscript Items Found Among Manuscripts," *American Archivist* 32 (no. 3, July 1970): 275-281.

Aural and Graphic
Archives and Manuscripts*

Ralph E. Ehrenberg

While increasing awareness and sophistication of historians and other researchers in the use of nontraditional communication formats is encouraging the development of audiovisual programs at an unprecedented pace, procedures have yet to be fully defined for administering aural and graphic archives and collections.

Nonscript, nonprint materials share several common characteristics of form and content that set them apart from traditional textual materials. First, their physical attributes differ markedly. Paper, film, glass, celluloid, metal, plastic and cloth are all used as physical mediums. Moreover, their size may vary from a few inches to over many feet in length, as in the case of right-of-way maps or panorama drawings, while their composition—"the way in which they were brought together"[1]—may include albums, scrapbooks, volumes, atlases, sets, or single items. Consequently, aural and graphic materials pose special (and often related) problems of handling, storage and preservation.

Second, the medium of expression is graphic or aural rather than script or print. Archivists and curators, as well as researchers, are limited to languages—the projections, scales and symbols of maps, the pictorial designs of posters, the magnetic configurations of sound records—which establish definite parameters of expression and interpretation. Third, they have technical and aesthetic qualities not found in traditional archives. A knowledge of art, science and technology is often required to evaluate and service them adequately. Fourth, subject content is highly varied, yet concentrated or individualized. Aural-graphic languages are used to illustrate, evoke and promote ideas, events, things, places or persons, thus raising complex problems of subject control and retrieval. Finally, their creation (compilation, editing, printing and

*The author is indebted to Nancy Malan and Leslie Waffen of the Audiovisual Archives Division, National Archives and Records Service, for their assistance in the preparation of the sections on photographic records and aural records, respectively.

processing) is generally a group process involving two or more persons. The cost of creation therefore often tends to "weed out" useless records.

While these common characteristics illustrate a general similarity among aural and graphic records, they also reflect significant physical and substantive differences that affect basic archival and curatorial functions. This paper will discuss these differences under the general headings of graphic, photographic and aural records.

Graphic Records

Graphics are a form of communication which expresses ideas by lines and symbols rather than words. They can be divided into two classes: scaled and unscaled. Scaled graphics are exact representations of selected features of the earth's surface (maps, charts and cartograms) or of individual objects (engineering and architectural plans). Unscaled graphics are pictures created manually or mechanically by drawing or painting, and include engravings, illustrated broadsides, historical pictures and posters.

In the small or medium-size archives and manuscript collection, two kinds of graphics should be retained permanently: 1) manuscript and printed or processed graphics on which manuscript changes, additions or annotations have been made for record purposes, and 2) printed or processed graphics that are attached or interfiled with other documents of record character. Because of basic differences in form and content, the latter should be removed and stored as separate physical entities or photographically reproduced. The argument for retaining the integrity of a file unit is a compelling one that goes to the heart of archival principles and there are enough unfortunate examples of the careless removal of graphics to make custodians wary of perpetrating similar errors. On the other hand, the substantive content of many graphics will undoubtedly be lost if preventive measures such as physical removal or reproduction are not undertaken. If oversized graphics are removed, the custodian should indicate that such a transfer has taken place either by leaving a transfer card in the place of the original or by attaching a list of the separated items to the series or collection inventory. Conversely, separated items also should be marked in pencil to identify the series or collection from which they were removed.

Arrangement

Graphics should be arranged intact as a group by agency of origin or donor, in their original order if possible. By maintaining original order, intellectual integration of graphics and textual documents is facilitated and the identification of untitled, unsigned graphics is made easier. When provenance and *respect des fonds* are disregarded and graphics from various sources are interfiled into a general geographical or subject scheme, integration and identification become increasingly difficult and often impossible.

If the original order cannot be determined below the series or collection level, scaled graphics should be arranged by geographic area (maps and charts) or by model or structure (engineering and architectural plans).[2] Further subdivisions by topic and date can also be added. Elaborate published classification schemes have been prepared for scaled graphics and may assist the custodian in selecting area or subject terms.[3]

The National Archives of the United States and the Pennsylvania State Archives arrange scaled graphics on an organizational basis consisting of a hierarchy of administrative and geographic levels. The following levels of arrangement are normally included in descending order: 1) a record group or subgroup composed of records of an administrative unit at the bureau level of government, 2) a series or subseries composed of records reflecting the divisional level of government, 3) a file unit consisting of an assemblage of related documents, and finally 4) individual documents. I have described the application of this approach to map arrangement more fully elsewhere.[4] An example illustrating the organizational approach is taken from the Pennsylvania State Archives:[5]

> **Record Group 12** Records of the Department of Highways
> **Subgroup** Bureau of Construction
> **Series** State Roads and Turnpikes
> **File Unit** Eastern (Portion of Pennsylvania)
> **Document** Individual Maps

Another way of arranging scaled graphics while maintaining provenance is according to function. The objective of the functional approach is to arrange and classify records according to the purposes for which they were created or accumulated. No hierarchical system need be devised; therefore, it does not require an extensive knowledge of administrative or donor history to arrange the material or to research in it. Another advantage in the case of official government records is that natural series arranged according to function do not have to be divided among several different record groups following each agency reorganization. The functional method seems particularly well suited for archives of reasonably small political and geographical units and manuscript collections.

Unscaled graphics differ markedly from scaled graphics. They do not generally pertain to any particular place or area and may include a variety of subjects, such as persons, things, phenomena and places. For these reasons, unscaled graphics whose original order cannot be ascertained should be arranged and described in a manner similar to photographic records.

Following arrangement, each graphic is "titled" in pencil (normally in the bottom right-hand corner of the verso) according to group or collection number, series, file unit and document number or date. Titled graphics should be stored unfolded in acid-free folders which are also titled in pencil with the appropriate identifier in the lower right-hand corner.

Retrieval

Because researchers are more interested in the subject content of graphics than in their organizational or functional relationships and because the subject content is so varied, graphics should be described individually or indexed graphically.

Descriptive elements vary according to type of graphic. For scaled graphics the elements generally include series or collection name, area or subject, title, author, date, scale (generally given verbally, "one inch to two miles," or in representative fractions, 1: 124,000), dimensions (height by width) and medium. Descriptive elements are essentially the same for unscaled graphics except that scale and area are not included.

A shelflist reflecting the arrangement scheme is useful as an internal finding aid for quick reference and initial research. The shelflist may be in page format and bound or in card format. Entries normally consist of the entry or file number, title fragment and date, but can be expanded to include substantially more detail, including content description and type of material. The most detailed lists include an interpretation or analysis and history of each graphic. Very few archives or manuscript collections have the staff or the funds to prepare analytical descriptions. This is the responsibility of the historian rather than the archivist or curator.

The conventional method for describing individual items is the catalog card. A properly designed card, cross-referenced by area, subject and author or artist, provides multiple access points to any document. For ease of reference, catalog cards can be color-coded: e.g., white for area, blue for subject, yellow for author/artist. Subject cataloging is time-consuming, but a well-conceived preprinted form that includes selected subject blocks which can be checked off to indicate subject content will facilitate processing.

Graphic or map indexes provide another method of controlling maps individually. Published outline maps can be color-coded to show the coverage of selected sets or series of maps and charts that cover a particular geographic region. Indexes can be bound by region or stored separately in folders. Visual and graphic catalog cards that include maps or pictures of documents also speed up processing and reduce handling of originals.

Although collective description is more applicable to textual records, it can be adapted for graphics if they are thoroughly indexed by area and subject. Traditional inventories are particularly useful when graphics and textual records are closely related but stored separately. A copy of each inventory can be annotated by the archivist or curator to show where each entry is stored.

Storage and Handling

Because of the nature of their origin (particularly scaled graphics), graphics have generally suffered some damage through use before the archivist or curator gets custody of them. The best and cheapest method of preservation is to place graphics in acid-free folders that are stored flat in standard map cases with sliding drawers no deeper than two inches, taking into account the heavy weight of full map cases. Floor weight load should be checked by a knowledgeable engineer to be sure that it will support the combined weight of oversized graphics and storage cases.[6]

Graphics must often be dissected to fit map cases although extremely large graphics should be rolled and stored in tubes. In no case should a graphic be folded. In time, acid deterioration along fold lines (which is easily observed by a brown, brittle appearance) will cause documents to literally fall apart.

Torn and deteriorated graphics should be reinforced and supported by acid-free rag paper, linen, nylon or muslin (attached by neutralized wheat flour paste or adhesive plasticized cellulose acetate foil laminated under heat and pressure) or enclosed in polyester (mylar) envelopes to strengthen them and prevent further tears and deterioration.

If extensive handling and use of certain individual graphics or series of graphics is anticipated, reference copies should be made. Since graphics are generally oversized, photostats or microfilm (70mm or 105mm) should be used in place of traditional forms of copying.

Photographic Records

Photographic records include all pictures that are produced on sensitized surfaces by the action of light and include still pictures, motion pictures and aerial photographs. Since motion pictures and aerial photographs are limited to a few specialized archives and manuscript collections, only still pictures will be discussed.

Because of the thousands of pictures produced daily, repositories must be selective in their retention policy. In general, pictures relating to the activities of an agency or donor, pictures having historical significance and pictures having value as works of art should be retained. Official pictures that can be disposed of are those that have had only a limited or one-time use, such as the thousands of photographs taken during a research project or identification photographs of large organizations.[7]

Arrangement

Photographic records consist of two forms: the original black-and-white negative or color transparency and the print. Normally, the negative or transparency is considered the record copy and the print a reference copy. In certain instances, such as purchased or donated photographs, the repository may only have a print. These unique prints along with annotated prints should also be considered record copies.

Aural and Graphic Archives

Since negative originals and unique prints are used for different purposes than reference prints, they should be stored and filed separately. The former should be used only for reproductive purposes. Continual use of originals and unique prints will result in damaging scratches, spots, and fingerprints. If they are valuable and frequently used, good quality copy negatives should be made. Ideally they should be housed in the photographic laboratory. At the very minimum they should be stored in closed stacks and restricted to staff use; in no instance should they be made available to casual researchers.

Negatives and unique prints should retain the original numbers assigned to them by the agency, firm or individual that produced them, and each series or collection should be maintained separately according to provenance and original order. Where order is lacking and it is not feasible to arrange by provenance, they may be arranged numerically simply by progressively registering each accession sequentially.[8]

A more sophisticated classification scheme has been devised by Paul Vanderbilt for the State Historical Society of Wisconsin. Each series or collection of negatives is assigned a Cutter code for the name of the series or collection originator or photographer:[9]

B 4	Bemis Collection
B 5	Billings Collection
•	•
•	•
•	•
B 58	Bittinger Collection

Individual film sheets are then assigned a unique control number by sequentially adding numbers to the series or collection number: B4-1, B4-2, B4-3. . . B4-n.

Each sheet of film should be stored in separate acid-free, sulphur-free envelopes that are sealed along the edge rather than down the center. Center seam adhesives of old negative jackets retain moisture which will stain and eventually destroy film emulsion.[10]

Both jacket and sheet film should be notated with the same negative number so that negatives will not become lost. The negative number can be hand-scribed on the film emulsion or photographed on a strip of high contrast sheet film which is attached to the sheet negative.[11]

Retrieval

Excessive handling eventually destroys negative originals and unique prints. To minimize handling, a good control system is imperative. A self-indexing reference print file that is keyed to the negative file should provide adequate intellectual control of the negative file.[12] Multiple point access to the print and negative file can be obtained by additional indexes and catalog cards arranged by subject.

To establish a self-indexing file, inexpensive photographic reference prints are made of significant original negatives and unique prints. These prints should be either placed in standardized (generally legal-size) acid-free, low-sulfur envelopes or dry mounted on 100 percent rag paper for support. Mounting is time and space consuming but provides good protection against curling and damage.[13] For convenience, copy negatives can be filed with prints, provided that they are stored in separate negative jackets.

The reference file can be organized according to four main categories: portraits, places, subjects, and events. While portraits are filed alphabetically by name of individual and generally pose few problems, the remaining three categories require the establishment of authority files to standardize retrieval terms. Special emphasis should be given to local subjects. For the geographical file, the custodian will find the references cited above for scaled graphics useful; for the subject file, the subject headings for the picture collection in the Newark Public Library are helpful.[14]

Each reference print or mount and corresponding envelope must be captioned for identification. The amount of information depends upon the category and level of retrieval desired, but all captions should include the file designation (Portrait File, Geographic File, etc.) title (subject/name/place/event), date of image, photographer, restrictions, provenance and negative number.

Determining the title and related caption information is sometimes difficult. Internal evidence that helps to identify textual and graphic records is often lacking. That is why it is important to arrange negative originals and unique prints according to provenance. Their organizational origins may help "to identify the time and place at which they were produced and the subjects to which they relate."[15] Another problem is that the historical significance of the subject content may differ from the photograph's original purpose. A classic example concerns a photograph made by the Office of Public Buildings and Grounds, a federal agency established to erect buildings and monuments in Washington, D.C. It is an image of two small children and their nanny, all three in high button shoes and prominent hats, the maid with her starched, ankle-length white apron. The photograph is filed by the agency of origin under Meridian Hill Park and captioned, "View showing texture of concrete in lower wall. Maid with small children in view."[16]

Captions can be typed on acid-free paper and dry mounted or hand written on the back of pictures or mounting boards. Pressure sensitive labels should not be used because the adhesives dry up and the labels fall off. To write on the back of a photograph, place the photograph face down on a sheet of glass and use a soft pencil.

Collective descriptions, such as inventories or guides, are useful for publicizing significant groups or collections. Standard descriptive procedures are recommended: a brief history of the photographic activity that produced the group or collection should be followed by the identification and description of the individual series.[17] Each entry should describe one series and these should be grouped either by administrative subdivision, by subject or by type.

Series entry descriptions should include a title line and descriptive paragraph. The title line consists of the subject to which the material relates, inclusive dates (as well as significant gaps), type of photographs and quantity. The descriptive paragraph should include information concerning the origin, subject and composition of the photographic series.

Storage and Handling

General storage and handling procedures have been mentioned above but special reference must be made to the problem of humidity and the storage of certain types of photographic negatives. Relative humidity should be maintained between 40 to 50 percent. Fungus growth is encouraged above 60 percent while film brittleness, curl and static charge result from very low humidity.[18] Temperature should be maintained at the same level that is recommended for other permanent records.

The three types of photographic negatives that require special attention are cellulose nitrate base film, glass plates and color transparencies. All three must be stored separately from "safety" or cellulose acetate base film which comprises the bulk of current film production.

Nitrate film in a deteriorated state is combustible and highly inflammable when tightly packed in envelopes or film cans and stored in a warm place. Cool temperatures and individual storage reduce the threat of deterioration and combustion, but it is still advisable to replace nitrate film with acetate copy negatives.

Nitrate base film can be identified by year of production and by testing. Most film produced during the period 1890-1930 (and aerial film from the late 1930s and early 1940s) was on nitrate base Paul Vanderbilt describes the procedure for testing nitrate base film:

> To identify nitrate film, cut a long thin sliver from a sample margin and touch a match to it. If it burns briskly with a yellow sparkling flame and leaves a crisp, black ash, it is nitrate; if it burns only slowly or goes out and leaves a whitish melted mass between the unburned part and the ash, it is acetate or safety film. Then examine the notching code and treat all films similarly notched accordingly. Safety film generally carries the imprinted word "safety" in the margin. Some films are not notched and hard to identify and there is such a thing as a laminate of safety and nitrate bases. With experience, one learns to tell the differences, in most cases, by appearance.[19]

Glass plates that have permanent value should be stored vertically either in archives boxes or envelopes separated by cardboard padding or in slotted plywood boxes. The weight of glass plate negatives poses a similar problem to the weight of map cases. Depending on the number of plates involved, it may be necessary to provide storage areas with reinforced flooring. When stored on shelving, glass plates should always be placed on the lower shelves to prevent toppling and to make handling less dangerous.

Color transparencies also require special attention. The organic dyes in color film are not permanent but will change less rapidly under cool storage conditions. Color film, therefore, should be stored at 40° F and 30 to 40 percent relative humidity for maximum protection. For security and references purposes, black-and-white copy negatives should be made.

Aural Records

Aural records are "sound-storing artifacts" that include a variety of sound recording and reproduction devices in the form of cylinders, discs and magnetic tapes.[20] Like other nonprint, nonscript material, sound recordings may complement the written or printed word (through rhetorical style, nuances and intonations) but they also have the quality to convey a "literal message," an attribute not found in any graphic medium.[21]

Most "sound archives" are primarily interested in mass-produced vocal recordings. The type of recording one is likely to find in an archives or manuscript collection, however, is likely to be unique spoken word or musical recordings. These should be retained particularly if they concern an activity or function of the agency of origin or donor. Examples of official sound recordings from the Oregon State Archives that have permanent value include proceedings of board and executive committee meetings, investigative reports, field notes, trip reports and oral presentations before courts and boards.[22]

Because o their rarity, Edward A. Colby also recommends that the following mass-produced vocal recordings be saved: early recordings (to 1909), "representative collections of early recordings as tangible or at least visible artifacts in the history of recorded sound," and out-of-print recordings.[23] Finally, all oral history sound recordings should be permanently retained even when a transcript is made, because most transcripts are not verbatim renderings of a tape.[24] They have often been edited both by the transcriber and the interviewer. Moreover, a typed transcript cannot reflect the tonal qualities of the voice.

Arrangement

Arrangement and classification schemes have not been standardized for aural records. Christopher Barnes briefly describes eight different methods of arrangement which can be grouped under three broad categories: numerical, provenance and thematic.[25] In numerical arrangement, each sound recording or accession is organized sequentially by number while thematic arrangement is alphabetically by subject, theme or event.

Arrangement by provenance poses special problems for sound recordings. Like photographs and unscaled graphics, aural records are generally created sporadically and do not necessarily reflect any special activity or function. Because of this, aural records in the custody of the Audiovisual Division of the National Archives of the United States are arranged by agency of origin and thereunder serially by number.

Retrieval

No commonly accepted format of description has been formalized. Basic elements of a sound recording consist of the physical artifact and the data recorded. Level of control depends upon the emphasis placed on each of these elements. Description of the physical artifact should include group or collection number, item number, title, date, type of sound recording, number of recordings (two-track, one side, etc.), time/footage and speed (7.5 inches per second, 33 rpm, etc.).

The descriptive element of an entry or catalog card should include information concerning the sound data's origin and general references to major subjects, themes and events. The latter is complicated by the necessity of using visual senses to interpret aural senses. In describing textual and graphic records, the archivist or curator can use written words and visual symbols to describe written words and visual symbols. But when verbal communication of sound recordings is "extracted for the purposes of description and identification, it must be transferred from one frame of sensory perception to another. This cannot be done without some loss of information."[26]

Description of individual sound recordings in the form of catalog cards or special lists is generally more useful than collective description. The latter, however, is helpful as a reference tool if organized around a series or collection, a subject or a theme, and is carefully indexed.

The retrieval of sound data is made more complex by the need to electronically reconvert the physical and magnetic configurations stored on various physical mediums into auditory symbols before they can be used.[27] Reconversion raises various technological and ethical problems.

Aural and Graphic Archives

Like photographic original negatives and prints, original sound recording cylinders, discs and magnetic tapes are fragile and will deteriorate with use. The data stored on the recordings, therefore, must be transferred from originals to duplicate copies that are used for reference and cataloging.

Available equipment for rerecording originals varies. Most authorities recommend professional recording equipment but portable home-use magnetic tape recorders/reproducers capable of rerecording high-fidelity sound on quarter-inch tape are satisfactory for the small or medium-size archives or collection. The type of tape most often recommended is polyester (mylar) magnetic tape because of its exceptional resistance to wear. Furthermore, polyester contains no plasticizing agents that can evaporate under certain conditions of humidity and temperature, leaving tapes brittle and weak.

Choices of tape speed, size and tracks still remain open to question. The Oregon State Archives rerecords on a reel-to-reel format at 3.75 ips while the National Archives uses 7.5 ips.[28] Reel size is also a problem. The larger the reel, the more economical. But a 10½ inch reel requires proportionally more access time than a smaller reel. The same is true of multiple-track recordings. While it is less expensive to use multiple-track recordings, access becomes more arduous.

Each duplicate tape should include a blank leader and trailer to reduce wear, facilitate threading and aid identification. It can be color-coded to identify master copies from reference copies or leaders from trailers. Identification should include the reel's identification number, recording speed and number of tracks. Finally, leaders and trailers should include a control signal, "recorded at a standard volume level, [to serve] as a basis for comparing and determining the condition of the tape in the future."[29] The control signal serves the same function as a microfilm grey or color scale.

Rerecording also enters the ethical realm. For instance, no effort beyond the correction of technical problems should be made to manipulate or distort the original sound, such as amplifying a weak voice. The value of sound rerecordings is in their ability to recreate the exact quality of the spoken or vocal voice. Of course, it is also unethical to edit by addition or deletion. Inadvertent breaks or tears in original recording tape should be flagged or noted by colored tape to warn the reader that an omission may exist.

Special equipment is also needed for reproducing or playback. A separate playback unit is recommended to eliminate the possibility of accidental or deliberate erasure. If this is not feasible, a combination recorder/reproducer should be modified by disconnecting the recording/erasing head. Earphones are also recommended so that other users will not be disturbed during playback.

Storage and Handling

Proper storage and handling are basic to the preservation of aural records; once they have been damaged, their content may be irretrievably lost. Because of the variety of materials, storage and handling techniques differ for each sound recording form.

Cylinder sound recordings were developed by Thomas Edison in the 1880s and produced until his death in 1931. There are two types: wax and celluloid. The wax type are particularly fragile and must be stored in a dry environment. Deterioration of wax cylinders, which results not from fungus but from moisture penetrating the wood flour, phenol gum cores, can be retarded by *avoiding* air-conditioned, humidified storage.[30]

Wax-type cylinders should be stored upright in fleece-lined boxes on cardboard tubes that permit the free flow of air around the cylinders and keep them from touching one another. Because of their fragile nature, they must not be stored in sliding drawers or handled by ungloved hands. The shock from sliding drawers and the heat of fingers can actually break the cylinders.[31]

Celluloid cylinders are hardier but should also be stored in an upright position on end and should not be allowed to touch one another. Celluloid cylinders are often distorted from cardboard inserts or plaster of paris linings that have swollen and disintegrated from dampness. These have to be cleaned and the distortion corrected before they can be rerecorded.[32]

There are four types of disc sound recordings: shellac, acetate, lacquer and vinyl. The acetate and lacquer discs are less durable than vinyl and shellac and should be handled and used accordingly. Glass was used as an acetate base during World War II and poses special problems because of its fragile nature. All large discs should be stored on end, on heavy utility shelves (although vinyl discs are lighter and can be stored on standard library shelving), supported by dividers and grouped by type to prevent warpage.[33] Vinyl 45 rps disc recordings may be stored in file drawers because of their light weight and for space economy.[34]

Magnetic tapes should be stored vertically on edge in their original containers on metal shelves. The accumulated weight of flat stacking may distort reels or damage tape edges. Exposure to magnetic fields, which can cause erasure, and ultraviolet light should be avoided. Temperature control and relative humidity should be the same as for discs and other archival documents. Magnetic tape should be loosely wound on reels to prevent physical tape distortion and print-through. Periodic playback (at least once every two years) will relieve strains on the tape.

Notes

1 T. R. Schellenberg, *The Management of Archives* (New York: Columbia University Press, 1965), p. 322.

2 Mary Larsgaard, "Map Classification," *Drexel Library Quarterly* 9 (October 1973): 38-39; Lyle F. Perusse, "Classifying and Cataloging Lantern Slides for the Architecture Library," *Journal of Cataloging and Classification* 10 (April 1954): 77-83.

3 U.S. Library of Congress, Subject Cataloging Division, *Classification, Class G: Geography, Anthropology, Folklore, Manners and Customs, Recreation,* 3d ed. with supplementary pages (Washington, D.C.: Government Printing Office, 1954; reprinted 1966), pp. 177-181; Samuel W. Boggs and Dorothy Cornwell Lewis, *The Classification and Cataloging of Maps and Atlases* (New York: Special Libraries Association, 1945); Roman Drazniowsky, *Cataloging and Filing Rules for Maps and Atlases in the Society's Collection,* rev. ed. (New York: American Geographical Society, 1969).

4 Ralph E. Ehrenberg, "Non-Geographic Methods of Map Arrangement and Classification," *Drexel Library Quarterly* 9 (October 1973): 49-54.

5 Interview with Martha L. Simonetti, Archivist, Pennsylvania State Archives, June 21, 1973.

6 Mary Galneder, "Equipment for Map Libraries," *Special Libraries* 61 (July-August 1970): 271-274.

7 Joe D. Thomas, "Photographic Archives," *American Archivist* 21 (October 1958): 421.

8 T.R. Schellenberg, op. cit., p. 328.

9 Paul Vanderbilt, "Filing Your Photographs: Some Basic Procedures," *History News* 21 (no. 6, June 1966): 5-6. Technical Leaflet 36.

10 George T. Eaton, "Preservation, Deterioration, Restoration of Photographic Images," *Library Quarterly* 40 (January 1970): 93.

11 Paul Vanderbilt, op. cit., p. 6.

12 Renata V. Shaw, "Picture Organization Practices and Procedures," *Special Libraries* 63 (October 1972): 448-456; (November 1972): 502-506.

13 Paul Vanderbilt, op. cit., p. 3.

14 William J. Dane, *The Picture Collection; Subject Headings,* 6th ed. (Hamden, Conn.: Shoe String Press, 1968).

15 T. R. Schellenberg, op. cit., p. 325.

16 Example suggested by Nancy Malan, Archivist, National Archives, September 12, 1974.

17 T. R. Schellenberg, op. cit., p. 339.

18 George T. Eaton, op. cit., p. 95.

19 Paul Vanderbilt, op. cit., p. 6.

20 Gordon Stevenson, "Discography: Scientific, Analytical, Historical and Systematic," *Library Trends* 21 (July 1972): 106-107.

21 Walter L. Welch, "Preservation and Restoration of Authenticity in Sound Recordings," *Library Trends* 21 (July 1972): 83.

22 James D. Porter, "Sound in the Archives," *American Archivist* 27 (April 1964): 328.

23 Edward A. Colby, "Sound Scholarship: Scope, Purpose, Function and Potential of Phonorecord Archives," *Library Trends* 21 (July 1972): 11.

24 Norman Hoyle, "Oral History," *Library Trends* 21 (July 1972): 73.

25 Christopher Barnes, "Classification and Cataloging of Spoken Records in Academic Libraries," *College & Research Libraries* 28 (January 1967): 49-52.

26 Gordon Stevenson, op. cit., p. 107.

27 Edward A. Colby, op. cit., p. 14.

28 James D. Porter, op. cit., p. 330.

29 Ibid., p. 334.

30 Walter L. Welch, op. cit., p. 91.

31 Ibid., pp. 92-94.

32 David Hall, "Phonorecord Preservation," *Special Libraries* 62 (September 1971): 357-358.

33 Walter L. Welch, op. cit., p. 95.

34 James D. Porter, op. cit., p. 334.

The Law and the Manuscripts Curator

Henry Bartholomew Cox

Note: Passage of the 1976 Copyright Act renders parts of Dr. Cox's article obsolete.

The law as it pertains to the administration and use of manuscript documents is an intriguing field whose basic principles it is the object of this brief survey merely to outline. Its complexities are the subject of careful analysis by copyright attorneys whose work over the past two decades has contributed to further refinements in the law, culminating in the hoped-for passage of a general revision in the law of copyright. Some of the most important but not necessarily all of the significant themes in the law which may confront the manuscripts curator are dealt with in this article, including literary property rights, deeds of gift, restrictions, photocopying, monetary appraisals, theft, and problems of slander and libel. What each archivist and curator should realize is that law definitely affects him or her in daily work either in the preparation of collections for public consumption or else in face-to-face dealings with the public.

Literary Property Rights

The archivist in a state or national government repository who deals primarily with records that are officially created as a function of public business usually has different kinds of legal restrictions placed upon him respecting the uses of the manuscript documents which he administers than does the manuscripts curator. The legal proscriptions against use which the archivist faces in such a situation are very often statutory, but ofttimes are the result of agency or departmental restrictions on use placed on the records at the time they were created or very shortly thereafter. In the case of the National Archives and Records Service, the custodian of the largest body of the official records of the United States Government, such restrictions on use as do exist are generally the result of administrative orders, but by far the preponderance of noncurrent materials housed in the National Archives building and in the Federal Records centers across the United States are freely available for public use and are not subject to donor restrictions as are many private collections which are offered to manuscript repositories, such as libraries and historical

The Law and the Curator

societies. The manuscripts librarian should thus begin to formulate a regularized policy with respect to gifts early in his practice, since a well-conceived policy regarding the literary property rights in acquisitions will pay big dividends later on.

What are these literary properties in manuscripts and why must they be acquired? Literary property is the intangible, but still very real, right of the author of any writing or his heirs to the first publication of that writing. Literary property is descendable and devisable, so that an author may will it either to his heirs or others whom he chooses. It is also subject to assignment, so that it may be sold or transferred to third parties. A writing does not need to be in a form specifically intended for publication and dissemination, such as a poem, short story or book, in order to be considered literary property and thus subject to common law copyright. Such historical manuscripts as letters, diaries, memoranda, and even rough notes or laundry lists are literary property whose physical manifestation in the form of paper, ink, envelope, and postage stamp may pass to an addressee, a subsequent bona fide purchaser, or a curator of manuscripts, without being accompanied by the right to publish or otherwise make available their contents.[1] According to the preponderance of decisions in the United States and foreign countries, unless the addressee, donee or purchaser obtains the permission from the author of a letter or similar document to publish its contents, he may not do so upon the author's death but must obtain the permission from the heirs of the decedent.[2] Heirs are quite frequently difficult to locate; and finding all of an author's living relatives, especially of an individual who has been dead for many years, is manifestly impossible. A manuscripts curator should realize that, as of this writing, he is subject to the impact of truly antique law, the common law of unpublished manuscript materials, conceived in the seventeenth and eighteenth centuries and applied today with surprisingly few changes in interpretation since that time.[3] This rule so strictly formulated in common law practice was intended to guard against invasion of privacy so that the right to written thoughts would inhere inviolate in the one who expressed them or his family, virtually as if the written words had never been uttered. One should note that, by comparison, this concept of "the dead hand" as it is currently applied to unpublished manuscripts disappeared, at least in principle, with respect to printed books at the time of the first United States copyright acts adopted pursuant to Article I, section 8, paragraph 8, of the United States Constitution; so that since 1789, authors of *printed* materials in which formerly unpublished manuscripts have been reduced to print have enjoyed the protection of copyright only "for limited times," and not in perpetuity.

With this background it appears obvious that the curator should obtain the services of an attorney to prepare a standard and brief deed of gift form to include the literary property rights in donated manuscripts and obtain assent to the donation of literary property whenever possible. Libraries would be well advised to urge donors to dedicate literary property rights in any and all manuscripts when they are first accessioned. Most libraries requesting surrender of such rights began to do so after World War II. The Chicago Historical Society and Louisiana State University have requested such rights for over 20 years; the Kentucky Historical Society, for 21 years; the State Historical Society of Wisconsin, for 18 years; and the Buffalo Historical Society, the Ohio Historical Society, the Illinois State Historical Library and the Utah State Historical Society, all for over 13 years. The Virginia Historical Society has been asking its donors to surrender literary property rights for over a century.[4]

In the above sense, literary rights are devisable, but the librarian must be careful to ascertain if there have been prior rights granted. The prospective grantor before the librarian may be but one of the owners of literary property in unpublished materials of an author; and through either a residuary clause or a division among family members in a share-and-share-alike provision of a will, other persons may have just as much right to the literary property as the willing donor and, what is more, may have already donated or devised the literary property. If, for example, an adult son or daughter of a writer sells or donates his or her share of inherited literary property to a corporation, an institution or an individual, or places it in the public domain, the rights of the mother or other children have passed at the same time, either with or without their consent.

As has been stated, discovery of legal heirs in order to obtain their permission to publish is frequently impossible. Professor Julian P. Boyd reported to the House Committee on the Judiciary on June 17, 1965, that his staff believed most courts would permit the technical invasion of literary property rights posed by publishing the letters to and from Thomas Jefferson. Believing that appropriate sanctions for their publication would be found in the "fair use" doctrine, the staff of the Papers of Thomas Jefferson has

The Law and the Curator

produced 19 peerless volumes whose world-renowned quality has long since justified their decision to publish. Other projects in both letterpress and microfilm sponsored by the National Historical Publications Commission have risked the threat of the possible recalcitrant heir in their faith that historical value—new light where before no knowledge has shone—would seem to justify publication over the sender or his descendants' objections. The sad fact for the historian is that, in some cases, the law has not recognized this possibility. "Fair use," or the permissibility of brief quotations for exposition, comment or criticism, does not apply to unpublished manuscripts, which are protected under common law copyright. The letters of James McNeill Whistler were lost to historians and the general public because Whistler's niece would not allow chosen biographers to publish them; and although the date of that decision was 1907, ample cases since have demonstrated the caution with which wise custodians have made their way through the common law thicket.

Thus, in administering manuscript collections in his custody, the curator may well ask himself the following questions: What rights does the historian or any author have to seek and to publish facts from unpublished manuscripts protected under common law? May the public's "right to know" in certain cases outweigh the private feelings of individuals? Is there a test which has been and may be successfully applied in the courts? Of course, the author has as much right to delve into the past for its value to the present as any investigator. Historians are by definition chroniclers; and so they must make both co-workers and the world beyond their fraternity aware of their discoveries. Such educated snooping is ill-calculated to win the warm approbation of those to whom it is an intrusion. Nonetheless, it continues to exist in the interest of scholarship, and it must persist, within the bounds of reasonable good taste, in order to advance the knowledge of our entire society. Researchers with an interest in primary sources will continue to investigate them in their belief that the public has a right to know. The opening of privately-held documentary resources to the scholar is entirely consonant with Thomas Jefferson's hope of 1791 that records should be preserved "not by vaults and locks which fence them from the public eye and use, in consigning them to the waste of time, but by such a multiplication of copies, as shall place them beyond the reach of accident."[5]

The perplexity and difficulty in giving the law's present answer to the unpublished manuscript dilemma is that the stringent common law rule in operation today is not amenable to research needs, but, curiously enough, in the future it appears inevitable that it will be altered in favor of increased liberality and greater precision as a result of the enactment of a proposed wholesale overhaul of the 1909 statute under which federal copyright now operates. What does the new copyright proposal do to meet the need of the archivist and historian? It appears to sharpen the definitions of permissibility to publish, to use and to teach from unpublished materials, so that both authors and custodians are better served. Upon passage of this statute, there would be assurance to the writer, the librarian and the publisher that 50 years after the death of the author of an unpublished document or 100 years after the writing of the document, the manuscript enters the public domain. If the manuscript, be it a laundry list or a love letter, is sold upon the autograph market or has been given or willed to a third party other than the immediate heirs of the creator of it, after the expiration of the statutory period it enters the public domain. If, therefore, the heirs of an author of a manuscript choose to "sit" on their own copy of the document and not to release it for research or publication, they may do so; but if another copy of the document exists and is in the hands of a researcher after the expiration of the statutory period, it could be freely published. The same would be true of a manuscript by the author which has come into the hands of a bona fide purchaser. The rationale of such statutory regulation in the field of personal letters is, of course, that a restriction of modest duration, figured from the time of the death of the writer, would reasonably protect the immediate interests and reputations of both the writer and his family, as well as persons mentioned or addressed in the manuscript. Researchers interested in publishing the information contained in historic letters would be able to do so after that time without fear of prosecution for infringement. Should a recalcitrant descendant appear at any time after the elapse of the statutory period and before publication, the burden would shift to the heir to demonstrate why such publication should not be allowed.[6]

Restrictions

Assuming that a donor does not wish free use of all of his papers and that the manuscript curator is willing virtually to provide a kind of storage service until a mutually-agreed time passes before access to them is permitted, there are a number of proper legal

The Law and the Curator

mechanisms which the curator may use. The collection may be entirely closed, in which case the legal significance is precisely what the term "closed" implies; namely, the curator is responsible to see to it that the manuscripts are physically separated from other materials and that after careful processing they are sealed or bundled up in such a way that even a curious staff member may not be tempted to pry into them. Part of a collection may be sealed, but this method of procedure is cumbersome and is not often used today because of the problems of administration to which it gives rise.

It is an understandable desire on the part of the librarian to want to accept important sealed material if he can encourage the donor to lift the ban within a reasonable period. Perhaps a person's lifetime plus 50 years is acceptable and fits within the spirit of the time lapse which precedes the entry of unpublished manuscript materials into the public domain, according to the presently proposed revision of the copyright act; but 25 years may be still more reasonable. Indeed, the ideal is to open collections to researchers as soon as possible, and donors should be encouraged to do so. But many curators are forced to place unfortunate restrictions on documents in their custody in order to secure them to their institutions or, in extreme cases, to prevent the putative donor from destroying them.

A collection which is subject to limited access provides the researcher some privileges within it, but still leaves the donor with the ultimate power of approval over the research product. The donor who wishes to put strings upon the use of his collection frequently does so by delegating the power of approval through a board of professional persons whom he deems qualified to pass upon the work, or may so delegate it to the curator. If a donor chooses to permit a single author to have first publication rights over the unpublished manuscripts, he may, of course, so specify at the time of the deed of gift or thereafter, but the curator should be aware of the fact that a so-called "court biographer" may attempt to tie up research materials indefinitely; and the curator should accordingly obtain a commitment from the donor proposing a definite period of termination for the first publication privilege or else be subject to a difficult problem of administration.

A librarian or archivist may self-impose restrictions on donated manuscripts, but is always subject to criticism for so doing or even possible legal action requiring him to state why particular materials should be censored or otherwise withheld from the research public's examination. If, however, the collection he accepts contains government classified materials, curators are wise to ascertain from the agency creating the documents if the same restrictions that were originally applied still pertain to them, since the unauthorized divulging of classified information, despite the Pentagon Papers case, may still bring about a stiff penalty depending upon the circumstances.

The fact that library restrictions do have teeth was illustrated in the celebrated Peter Kavenagh case in New York, in 1960.[7] Letters of John Quinn received by the New York Public Library under the proviso that they not be published until 1988 were set to be published by Kavenagh in a pirated edition which the court ordered destroyed. Similarly, the London Library permitted Phyllis Grosskurth access but no right to quotation to the memoirs of John Addington Symonds. These are but two recent examples of extreme reluctance on the part of libraries to permit publication in violation of the spirit of a restricted gift, despite the wish of authors to disseminate ever more in-depth information about the subjects of their inquiry or even the barely suppressed desire of manuscript librarians to see to it that the author's wishes could be realized.

Yet another interesting case shows the reliance of a court upon the publication of original documentation. It presents the irony of the court's not only permitting, but also demanding, exhibit—and thus publication—of manuscript letters and documents bearing upon the character of an individual. This was the case of Helen Clay Frick versus Dr. Sylvester Stevens.[8] Dr. Stevens published a work which described Miss Frick's father, Henry Clay Frick, as "brusque and autocratic," a judgment which many historians felt was a generous one. Nonetheless, Miss Frick sought an injunction against the book's further distribution. According to the text of the *New York Times* article of July 23, 1965, reporting the progress of the case at Carlisle, Pennsylvania, "Judge Weidner ruled . . . that the defendant would have to produce original source materials as evidence to support his contention that the book's account of Mr. Frick was truthful." The production of such evidence involved publication to the extent of being included in the court record; and this publication was mandatory—without the approval of Frick's daughter.

The Law and the Curator

Photocopying

Is the act of photocopying and xeroxing of manuscript materials covered under common law protection? Again, comment upon this thorny issue may well revolve around what a court is *likely* to do as opposed to what it is empowered by the application of existing legal principles to do in fact. A single copy of a manuscript item made solely for the purposes of study or research will probably be viewed by any court which has analyzed the Court of Claim's opinion in *Williams and Wilkins Co. v. The United States (1973)* as constituting no publication within the meaning of the law. Although the Williams decision specifically treats those cases involving photocopies of copyrighted material made for distribution without the publishers' permission, the spirit of the decision is a landmark in the copyright field. The court ruled that since Congress has left the problem of photocopying untouched in the copyright laws, it would give the benefit of the doubt "to science and the libraries, rather than to the publisher and the [copyright] owner. . . . "[9] Courts, in other words, are quite likely to permit scholars the fair use of both unpublished manuscripts and copyrighted works at the present time, and a strong reason for their change in the common law viewpoint toward uncopyrighted material, even before the passage of the copyright law revision, is the able representations before House and Senate committees which were made by archivists, librarians and historians in the 1960s, at which time their important testimony caused key language to be added to the copyright revision bill. The pertinent language in the bill dealing with fair use now provides that:

> . . . the fair use of a copyrighted work, including such use by reproduction in copies or phonorecords or by any other means specified [elsewhere in the bill] . . . for purposes such as criticism, comment, news reporting, teaching, scholarship, or research, is not an infringement of copyright. In determining whether the use made of a work in any particular case is a fair use, the factors to be considered shall include:

> 1 the purpose and character of the use;
> 2 the nature of the copyrighted work;
> 3 the amount and substantiality of the portion used in relation to the copyrighted work as a whole; and
> 4 the effect of the use upon the potential market for or value of the copyrighted work.[10]

Also included in the language of the bill is a section dealing with reproduction of works in archival collections, which asserts that:

> . . . it is not an infringement of copyright for a library or archives, or any of its employees acting within the scope of their employment, to reproduce no more than one copy or phonorecord of a work, or distribute such copy or phonorecord, under the conditions specified by this section and if:
>
> 1 the reproduction or distribution is made without any purpose of direct or indirect commercial advantage; and
>
> 2 the collections of the library or archives are (i) open to the public, or (ii) available not only to researchers affiliated with the library or archives or with the institution of which it is a part, but also to other persons doing research in a specialized field. . . .[11]

So it seems that even before the copyright bill is passed, libraries and manuscript repositories are becoming more willing to furnish single copies of materials in their possession, but are warning the recipients of the existing limbo in which the law relating to unpublished manuscripts will remain until the revision statute is enacted.

It virtually goes without saying that, as a matter of ethics, etiquette, and common sense, borrowed manuscripts in a repository should not be photocopied for a researcher or displayed in an exhibition without the lender's permission, even though the lender may not be holder of the literary copyright. The owner of the physical document itself, although not possessed of the literary rights, still has the power to donate, sell, retain, exhibit, or even to destroy the document; so, it is obvious that the owner should be consulted before the tangible item itself is displayed or reproduced in any way. Any unauthorized copying is, therefore, a reduction in the property in the item which the owner possesses; and it should not be permitted without the owner's consent.

Appraisal

One of the most prolific sources of "legal troubles" for manuscript curators need not be unduly burdensome if librarians or archivists are willing to summon the help of professional colleagues early and work with them carefully. This is the matter of appraisal or valuation of donated manuscripts. There are many

The Law and the Curator

points to be learned in this complex field, but three rules stand uppermost: 1) be aware that the law has changed and probably will continue to change; 2) consult an attorney or an appraiser for specific help when you need it; and 3) realize that ways to establish values do exist and are a useful start even for an amateur in the field.

The law, indeed, has changed. In 1969, the tax reform act did away with the fair market value of literary property at the time of an author or composer's gift. In other words, before 1969 if a writer's donated papers would bring $2 million if sold, he could use the full amount as a deduction of his income tax return. This is no longer the case.

> According to Section 1221 (3) of the Internal Revenue Code, such things as music manuscripts, literary manuscripts, letters, memoranda, and similar property, when still in the hands of the person whose personal efforts created the property, are no longer entitled to this treatment. If a composer wants to give them away to a library, the law holds that these properties cannot be considered capital assets. They must be considered ordinary income properties, and as such, their value is established on a cost basis.[12]

This means that, after making his gift, the author or composer may get little more credit for his largesse than the value of the paper and ink, regardless of the fair market value. The intent of the framers of these amendments was to make it impossible for former statesmen, such as presidents and political leaders, to claim large income tax deductions by making gifts of their personal papers to presidential libraries or other manuscript repositories. Although the proponents of tax reform, it may be assumed, had no special animus towards authors and composers (to say nothing of libraries), the result of their work has been to penalize creators and to wreak havoc with acquisitions policies in scholarly institutions. In the midst of this dilemma, resulting in a much reduced donation of manuscripts to many of the major repositories, prospective donors to the Library of Congress are carefully warned that gifts of self-created manuscripts may not be a benefit tax-wise, and they are furnished with a copy of the General Counsel's "Memorandum on the Tax Reform Act of 1969," plus the gentle hint that it might be well to seek professional advice. Assuming the donor is not the creator but his heir (ironically the deduction, if any, may only be enjoyed by someone other than the author), a librarian will then inescapably face the question of establishing a valuation on the collection, if not for the sake of the donor's tax deduction, then certainly for the purpose of insurance.

Most repositories either employ professional appraisers or instruct their donors to do so. The wise archivist or curator will not attempt to appraise materials for receipt into his or her own institution, both for self-protection and for protection of the donor should the Internal Revenue Service question the amount and type of the gift.[13] Assume at the outset that there are few if any loopholes which federal tax experts have not at least discovered, if not plugged, and be judicious and deliberate. Hire a specialist in appraisal work, such as a dealer in manuscripts, if it is not possible to employ one of the extremely few individuals in this world whose life work is solely document appraisal. The names of several qualified firms or individual manuscript dealers may be obtained through the secretary of the The Manuscript Society. If a collection is small, a professional manuscript appraiser is an expensive luxury in relation to the per piece cost of his appraisal. In that case, it may be possible for an individual custodian to do some preliminary research of his own in *American Book Prices Current* and in the "prices-realized" columns of recent major autograph action catalogs. This research would not be undertaken in an effort to become an instant "expert" on manuscript pricing and values, which is virtually impossible for a librarian because of the wide latitude in types of manuscript documents and their contents and the experience required to become such an expert, but it would be an effort to dredge up background pricing information in order to minimize the time that a professional appraiser, who may not be familiar with autograph letters but who is qualified to appraise antiques or objects of art generally, may have to spend evaluating several discrete items. This man's appraisal on his own letterhead, so long as it has been an honest effort to arrive at a fair market value and shows some justification in terms of background references to similar sale items, is frequently as competently researched and referenced as the appraisal of a manuscripts expert, and will rarely be attacked by Internal Revenue.

Theft

There are many kinds of physical security for manuscript documents, such as proper provision of acid-free folders and boxes, and fire protection by sprinklers. Violation of the elementary principles of these will rarely involve the transgressor in any legal

The Law and the Curator

consequences. A significant area in which definite legal aspects do pertain, however, is the question of the stolen manuscript and what to do with it.

Institutions may, of course, devise the best preventive techniques money can buy but they will not entirely prevent thefts or attempts at theft. Of course, I hardly need emphasize that the librarian should know well the source from whom he buys. If he gets a stolen document by purchase from a dealer, the dealer bears the loss; but if it is obtained from a thief, the librarian takes his chances of getting even a partial return of his original investment in the document, since the thief rarely if ever has money to cover the purchase price.

Theft may never be entirely avoided, but there can at least be intelligent attempts to minimize it or control it. One of the methods often used is that of stamping manuscripts with a distinctive device which is easily recognizable. This method of operation may be practical when one is dealing with only a few documents, but is almost out of the question if the librarian or archivist is dealing with items in the thousands or even millions. A stamp is similar to a brand in that it enables the authorities to return estrays to their proper owners with a minimum of difficulty. Aside from stamping techniques, virtually nothing takes the place of a well-policed search room: one in which the searcher is supervised in his use of documents without being smothered. It is difficult for the manuscripts curator to achieve that almost mystical balance between virtually no supervision and a sense of authoritarianism or intense surveillance over the shoulder of the worker among his collections, but the best institutions somehow seem to have it.

Legally, it is fully permissible for an institution politely to request searchers to open briefcases or handbags upon their departure. In an analogous situation, a recalcitrant patron in a store or shop may be subject to search, particularly if there exists reasonable belief on the part of a salesperson that the individual in question has stolen or shoplifted any goods. So far as is known, however, the brief period of detention for a discreet search, known in tort law as "shopkeeper's privilege," has not been extended from stores or sellers of commodities in shops to keepers of manuscripts, and a custodian would need to be wary of conducting any such search himself. A reasonably quick and prudent solution to most situations in which it appears obvious that the custodian will make a formal charge is to summon the authorities, preferably

The Law and the Curator

while the suspect visitor is still on the premises, and then to question him or her out of the presence of others in the search room. It is highly important, in view of the possibility of error, to minimize the institution's chances of being sued for false arrest; but it is nonetheless a curator's privilege and duty toward his honest clientele and to the public at-large to protect the materials which his institution holds in trust, and to defend them against loss through dishonesty. The law will thus uphold the custodian's reasonable good-faith efforts to enforce the security of his institution.

Slander and Libel

If the manuscripts custodian conducts an oral history program, or has taped interviews in a collection along with manuscripts which pertain to the interviews, he should be aware of the elements of the tort rules of slander and libel, since potential legal difficulties are present if oral materials are not carefully used. Generally speaking, *libel* is written defamation; *slander* is oral, in the presence of a third person. But an interviewee on tape, although orally expressing himself, commits libel if he defames someone, since he has done so in a permanent form of expression. What are the constituent elements of defamation? Usually statements will be deemed libelous which: 1) demean an individual in his business or profession; 2) assert that he is a mental defective or the victim of a vile or communicable disease; 3) subject the individual to scorn or ridicule; or 4) attack his reputation. Defenses to these allegations do exist; namely, 1) that the statement can be proven to be true; 2) that it was made in the course of a legal proceeding by one of the parties at the proceeding; or 3) that it was fair comment upon a matter of public interest, such as a news writer's story on a broad and difficult social problem, so long as the statement is made without malice.

The curator's best course would obviously be to audit those items in his collections that might contain libelous statements and so warn his users that publication of them might involve legal consequences. He should study the libel laws of his state, but preferably consult with the lawyer for his institution in order to explore possible ways and means of negating the impact of potential legal action against the institution by such devices as a pre-use statement to be signed by the researcher, warning him of the consequences of publication of libelous remarks. By taking the trouble to advise an author or his publisher of the difficulties involved in the use of such material, the curator will not absolutely be insulated against a suit (and it is, indeed, scant comfort to learn that a plaintiff in a libel action does not usually get the sum he asks). Still, by this or a similarly careful course of action, the judicious custodian will have done virtually all he can to prevent major problems.

Conclusion

The preceding summary of selected subject areas in which law and the librarian may come face-to-face is intended only as an introduction to some of the more recurrent confrontations and must not be mistaken for the careful advice of a trained and licensed attorney. Part of its purpose is to emphasize the ever-changing and increasingly complex nature of this area of the law, crossing as it does the disciplines of tort, contract, administration of decedants' estates, wills, literary property and copyright, federal estate and gift taxation, and remedies. Of course, as has been emphasized, the law of literary property as it affects scholars and custodians will undergo its most important changes in several hundred years when passage of the copyright revision is achieved.

It would seem that the essential interests of archivists and manuscript librarians have been safeguarded in the new copyright laws. The enthusiastic desires of historical researchers, while subjected to some uncertainties until such time as it is possible to foresee the final provisions of the law, are not likely to be grievously damaged. Archivists and historians alike may, in the end, have to accept certain inconveniences in order to have others lightened. The more than 20 years of research, of hearings, and of legislative give-and-take that have been required to forge a new copyright law provide a lively example of the adjustments that a modern society must make within itself in order to come to terms with technological progress. And perhaps even more significantly, this process provides a prime example of the way in which a democratic society works to reconcile conflicting interests, and to arrive at compromise solutions that will strengthen rather than weaken the fabric of society. It has been both challenging and instructive for archivists and librarians in the United States to be involved in this process. Together, they will continue to press forward to provide maximum historical documentation to authors—manuscript materials which will have a distinct bearing upon the future of historical interpretation.

Notes

1 Right to publish does not inhere originally in the recipients of letters, nor does it obtain in subsequent purchasers. See Harry Ransom, "The Personal Letter as Literary Property," in *Studies In English,* vol. 30 (Austin: University of Texas Press, 1951), pp. 116-131.

2 "Personal Letters in Need of a Law of their Own," *Iowa Law Review* 44 (1959): 705-715. This takes cognizance of the historian's plight, especially with regard to recent material. See Philip Wittenberg, *The Law of Literary Property* (Cleveland: World Publishing Co., 1957), p. 76, which underscores the problems of the biographer and historian; J. L. Wilson, "The Scholar and the Copyright Law," *ASCAP Copyright Symposium,* no. 10 (1959), p. 104; and L. R. Yankwich, "What is Fair Use?" *University of Chicago Law Review* 22 (1954): 203. Wilson's treatment is particularly significant in the area of manuscripts at pp. 113-121.

3 The first major reported cases are *Pope v. Curl* 2 Atk. 342, 26 Eng. Rep. 608 (Ch. 1741) and *Thomson v. Stanhope,* 2 Ambler 737 (Ch. 1774).

4 Henry Bartholomew Cox, "The Impact of the Proposed Copyright Law upon Scholars and Custodians," *The American Archivist* 29 (no. 2, April 1966): 222-223.

5 *Report to the President Containing a Proposal by the National Historical Publications Commission* (Washington: 1963), pp. 8, 29.

6 Henry Bartholomew Cox, "Private Letters and the Public Domain," *The American Archivist* 28 (no. 3, July 1965): 387.

7 Cox, "The Impact of the Proposed Copyright Law Upon Scholars and Custodians," *The American Archivist* 29 (no. 2, April 1966): 223.

8 Loc. cit.

9 *Williams and Wilkins Co. v. United States,* 485 F. 2d 1345, 1359 (1973).

10 S. 644, "A Bill for the General Revision of the Copyright Law, Title 17 of the U. S. Code," section 107 (1971).

11 Ibid., section 108.

12 Irving Lowens, "Why Tax Reform Should be Reformed,"*Manuscripts* 23 (no. 3, Summer 1971): 186.

13 Seymour V. Connor, "A System of Manuscript Appraisal," *History News* 22 (no. 5); *American Association for State and Local History,* Technical Leaflet 41 (May 1967). See also Ralph G. Newman, "Tax Problems of the Collector," *History News* 20 (no. 10); *American Association for State and Local History,* Technical Leaflet 31 (October 1965).

Archival Preservation

Clark W. Nelson

Archival custodians deal with two elements in their attempts to preserve the past. The first is the physical state of the document itself; the second is the environment in which it is stored. The skill with which the preservationist balances these will determine his success in keeping his collection safe from future degradation. Unfortunately, this activity requires money and expertise. In the case of document repair, the expenditures can be considerable and time-consuming. The archival neophyte should not, however, despair if he lacks sufficient resources or does not have the most modern of facilities. He can do much by applying good sense and judgment to his limited situation. It is hoped that this brief resume will help keep one's direction true despite whatever frugalities are necessary. One should be mindful of the fact that it is important to not only build a collection of high research value but also one that will endure because of its physical well-being.

In the past, the archivist has not been alone in his concern about the preservation of paper. He has had allies who through tradition and experience developed skills in the conservation of rare books and artistic works. Regrettably, the major efforts to understand the deterioration of paper scientifically have been made in this century. During this period, the important studies have all been conducted since World War I. Today there is a movement to better educate and train people interested in the specifics of preservation. Recently the Society of American Archivists, the National Archives, and the National Bureau of Standards have been sponsoring a research program on the stability of archival materials. For a number of years, the Council on Library Resources has funded one of the most successful attempts to solve paper and book problems at the W. J. Barrow Research Laboratory, Inc., in Richmond, Virginia. The International Institute for Conservation of Historic and Artistic Works (IIC), the American Institute for Conservation (AIC), and within the past year, the National Conservation Advisory Council have all been providing guidance in preserving historic material.

It is the responsibility of archival custodians to support such at-

tempts to better understand the historic materials they are preserving. It is also important that they recognize the need to be
kept informed in this area of growing knowledge. Journals, such
as the *American Archivist,* now regularly feature articles and news
notes on recent developments in this field. Journals of the
aforementioned conservation societies also contain related articles on the current scene.

Environmental Control

The ability to control the environment in today's archives is an
important contribution of modern heating/cooling technology.
Unfortunately, there are still those who are not blessed with full
controls. Ideally, one should be able to maintain a temperature of
65° F to 75° F, along with a humidity of 50 to 55 percent. Those
without the mechanical ability to adhere to the recommended
ranges may be able to add portable humidifiers or dehumidifiers
to supplement their systems.

Whatever the individual environmental limitations are, every attempt should be made to hold to the norms. The deviations that
are allowed should minimize temperature and humidity extremes.
Frequent cycling of temperature/humidity is also to be avoided.
Paper records can handle, in most cases, a greater variation from
the recommended standard than plastic-based records: photographs, motion pictures, tapes, microfilms, etc. The special conditions for these materials will be dealt with later.

In recent years, the problems of pollution in our urban areas have
created additional preservation hazards. The acids and particles
generated by smoke, exhaust, etc., have made it necessary to
install other devices that filter the air by washing or electrostatic
means. The new Madison Building of the Library of Congress
features a washed air system. While the archivist cannot do much
about the quality of the outside air, he can control the pollution
caused by his staff and researchers. For example, a restriction on
smoking in stacks and search room areas will reduce it and
minimize fire hazards as well. A prohibition against eating in
these key areas will also minimize the defacement of documents
by insects searching out food particles. For these reasons, a
smoking/eating room well away from the stacks with separate
ventilation is a desirable feature of any archival facility.

The illumination in the archives is another factor affecting record life. Before the energy crunch, rooms were lit up like sunny beaches. Fortunately, we now find that lower levels of illumination do the job just as well. The archivist must, nevertheless, be on guard for damage by the ultraviolet rays from his lights. Of particular concern are documents on display. Here definite rotation policies should be established and wherever possible, copies should be used or filters of yellow plastic installed over the lights or the documents. Unfortunately, the most economical of lights, the fluorescent, causes the worst fading. Fortunately, extruded plexiglass filters are available in museum supply houses that will reduce their damaging ultraviolet waves. These can be slipped directly over the fluorescent tubes. Satisfactory results can also be obtained by using yellow Kodagraph sheeting supplied by Eastman Kodak Company. When using filters, one should not forget that they, too, fade and need periodic changing. In recent years, fluorescent tubes have been introduced whose ultraviolet rays have been reduced. These would be preferred. The tungsten bulb is still a good investment in terms of its radiation hazards. It is not nearly as damaging as the fluorescent, and it does create shadow areas which tend to liven up our evenly lit rooms. From the foregoing, one can deduce that unnecessary illumination in any form is not to be encouraged. Stacks and search rooms should not have windows for two reasons—unwanted ultraviolet light, and better security.

Security and Natural Disaster Precautions

Security is another important aspect of preservation. Any archival facility needs safeguards to insure that a document will remain in the collection. A plan should be developed to keep the storage areas secure at all times. Restricted access, locked doors, and other sensible measures should be employed.

Adequate fire alarms need to be installed. The early smoke and heat detection systems are receiving increasing use. Fire and water are still the major hazards of historical collections. Reviewing one's needs with a trained fire engineer will pay big dividends if a conflagration occurs.

In recent years, flood and rain water has damaged archives and museums across the United States. Examining one's location in relation to a possible natural disaster is an important part of developing a preservation program. If flooding is a real possibility, steps should be taken to insure that the most valuable items are kept in areas above potential flood lines. All personnel should have knowledge of what to do with water-damaged materials. The Library of Congress has developed some excellent material on the subject. In areas where natural disasters do not normally occur, consideration should be given to the possibility of broken pipes in plumbing or malfunctioning fire prevention systems. The significant point to remember in such situations is that prompt action is of primary importance. The quicker one attacks the problem, the greater the chances of saving the collection.

Handling Practices

One of the important aspects of archival preservation is the development of handling practices that will further the longevity of the collection. As mentioned earlier, cleanliness offers many benefits. This should be carried further by emphasizing to one's staff the care of their hands and their surroundings. Separate work tables in areas away from storage rooms will do much to keep the normally dirty task of cleaning and organizing records from contaminating those already boxed. If one can afford a cleaning table with an exhaust, so much the better. Many, though, utilize a conventional table with room for sorting and cleaning records.

Upon arrival in an archives, most records need not only arranging but cleaning. Their prior storage conditions usually are not conducive to cleanliness. Consequently, dust, dirt and even insect life will be found. Before adding such materials to the collection, they must be cleaned. Soft brushes made of sable, etc., can be used for this purpose. It does not take long to recognize that brittle, frayed documents lose pieces easily unless gently handled. Soft erasers can also be used to minimize dirt, etc. A most effective cleaner is that used for wallpaper. It is kneaded like dough and gently drawn over the surface of a paper document from its center out. The document is held firmly during the process to prevent damage. The cleaner will easily remove much grime. There is one caution. Care must be taken to keep the small flecks of cleaner from remaining on the document before it is boxed.

Vacuum cleaners can also be of assistance in the cleaning process, but they must be handled carefully. A nylon stocking placed over the suction tube will reduce the possibility of drawing weak pieces of paper into the canister. The lowest possible suction must be used, and the especially weak and brittle materials avoided. If a reverse (blowing) action is available, it can sometimes be more useful. With large quantities of materials in both boxes and stacks, one can then quickly remove great quantities of the looser dirt and dust. A compressed-air hose coupled with an exhaust provision on a hooded table is the ultimate. For those handling large numbers of materials, varied or otherwise, it is a blessing. Records, books, artifacts, etc., can all be quickly and easily dusted with such equipment.

After cleaning, the question of insect life and mildew should be considered. In humid climates, this will be routine consideration. No matter where one lives, however, the tendencies to store records in almost every cubbyhole, whether in institutions or dwellings, usually produces some evidence of insect interest or mildew involvement. Exposure to sunlight and a good airing can be beneficial. Obviously, with the possibilities of further fading, this approach is not the best. Rather, fumigation by the use of a simply constructed box containing thymol is one of the easiest and least expensive approaches for small quantities of materials. Though lacking in permanency, thymol can be an effective sterilizer. The items needing attention are placed in a cabinet where the chemical is melted in watch glasses by the heat of 25-watt bulbs. In the case of insect life, a saucer of paradichlorobenzene crystals (1.5 oz. per cubic foot of air space) is placed in the cabinet and the contents sealed shut for two weeks.

The length of time required, coupled with the difficulty of penetrating the centers of books and stacks of paper documents with the vapors, makes the above approach a poor processor for large quantities of materials. For these, the vacuum method is recognized as the most efficient and effective. Its equipment costs, until recently, have been near the $10,000 mark. Within the last few years, a small unit has been developed which sells for around $3,000. It will fumigate a small cart of books and papers within a matter of hours. Fumigation cabinets designed for furriers have also been used for large quantities of documents. Since they operate without the benefits of a vacuum, they are slower and less efficient.

After cleaning and fumigation comes the task of boxing the materials. Here one can use a number of handling techniques that will minimize wear and strain on the paper documents. All sheets should be unfolded and boxed flattened out. Folds which are particularly stubborn or sheets that are badly wrinkled can be flattened by first humidifying them and then gently ironing at a low heat setting. Care must be taken to avoid wetting the inks and causing them to bleed or transfer. A simple press can also help the flattening process.

When handling documents, avoid the use of pressure-sensitive tapes. The dark brown stains from the older tapes should provide ample warning. While it is true some of the newer products are superior, they still offer hazards that make them undesirable. If documents are torn or separated, either leave them that way or earmark them for the attention of a restoration expert. If tape is still your choice, always use it on the reverse side, not on the side of the writing. But think twice before resorting to such an expedient. Any future restoration of the document will be made more difficult, if not impossible, by such action.

Before boxing, remove rubber bands, clips and staples. If staples are used, those made of rust-free stainless steel are best. Keep aged, badly stained papers separated from the others by interleaving sheets of acid-free paper between them. Such deteriorating papers should, ideally, be separated and duplicates inserted in their place. If their value warrants, they should be scheduled for deacidification and restoration.

Currently there are a number of storage boxes available that are acid-free in construction. These are highly recommended. While it is true some repositories use boxes of a low-acid nature, this practice has its hazards. The so-called records center boxes usually fall into this category. One must remember that they are designed for relatively short-term storage, and while cheaper in cost, do encase documents in a less desirable environment.

The use of acid-free folders is also recommended. Here again, there are also low-acid types available. These should be avoided if possible. If the budget is low, however, the low-acid folder is preferable to the regular kind. The more acid-containing materials we bring together in storage, the more difficult our preservation task becomes. Whenever possible we should try to upgrade our storage containers and file folders to the acid-free type.

There are now available on the market alkaline papers that contain a buffering agent which reduces the chances of future acid development. Permalife is one of these. It is available in several forms, such as folders, boxes, etc. It is a highly recommended paper for long-life use. For those needing a long-life writing paper, it can be readily substituted. Permalife's longevity is projected in the centuries. It is one of the developments from re-search conducted since World War II in paper.

When boxing and shelving paper documents, the boxes should be full or their sheets blocked up so that they stay flat. Most boxes today are designed to store paper vertically. This method is usually satisfactory, provided the documents are not allowed to sag in their containers. A few archives store their papers horizontally. This does eliminate sagging and other strains on the paper. There are special boxes available for this purpose. Such boxes as the Hollinger can be laid horizontally on the shelf so their contents remain flat. Unless one has specially constructed boxes, they cannot normally be stacked in such a position. Despite the larger shelf space required, horizontal storage is still a desirable method and can be used even in a smaller facility for valuable items of a limited number.

Before committing documents to permanent storage, each archivist faces the major question of why he is doing so. It is well to note that at this point one should also examine all possible alternatives to storing the documents intact. If the items are fragile and difficult to use, it is possible that microfilm or xerographic copies would be a better choice. The originals can then be permanently stored and the copies made available to the searcher.

This same approach can be used as a collection ages. At any time, duplicate copies will help preserve originals. In certain cases, the copy can become the "original" if other factors have become so persuasive. Miniaturization is part of today's archival world. Many of our materials come to us that way. It is important to remember that we can use such a method to further preserve older, more valuable and fragile collections. While preservation is mainly concerned with an original document, we as custodians of the past must make every effort to preserve the information it contains for as long as it is physically possible, in whatever form offers the longest life.

Preservation of Plastic Base Materials

Up to this point, emphasis has been given to paper documents. In modern-day archives, there has developed another class of materials of great significance. These are broadly known as audiovisual documents. All of these share one thing in common, they generally have a plastic base. This plastic may be cellulose acetate, polyester, etc. Motion pictures, recordings, microfilm and photographs are all important parts of the audiovisual breakdown. The fact that these materials have some form of plastic base makes their preservation problems similar.

In recent years the stability of plastics in general has been improved considerably. New formulations have been developed, and the earlier tendencies to embrittlement and shrinkage have been minimized. There is, nevertheless, still a need to be vigilant about giving plastic-based materials a more controlled storage environment. While a temperature of 70° F with a 50 percent relative humidity will be satisfactory for all forms of plastic-based records, authorities will vary in specific recommendations for such materials as microfilm (65° F to 70° F with 40 percent humidity), etc. In general, the concerns are focused on not too high or too low temperatures and humidities. Mildew can rapidly occur at one end of the scale and embrittlement at the other. The goal is consistency in the recommended storage environment.

In photographic applications, color images will be found. The stability of the dyes used in them is particularly questionable. The earlier color materials often exhibit a marked change in their colors. The newer films are considered more stable, but the fading tendency remains. One should be mindful of this and keep these materials away from ultraviolet light, while also making certain that their environment is the best available to the archives. With color materials, it is well to have a black-and-white copy available as a backup against fading.

Some photographic materials use glass as their base. In these situations, great care should be taken in their handling and storage. Special individually-slotted boxes can be purchased for the storage of glass plates or slides. Whatever method is finally chosen, the danger of breakage must be ever guarded against.

In the audiovisual field, the storage container should, like the carton for paper storage, be made of the best available materials, preferably with no acid. Microfilm and motion picture film has been found to develop microscopic blemishes from paper storage containers. Cans or inert plastic containers are recommended for them. Negative envelopes and print folders, etc., should all be made of acid-free papers.

The reels of tape recordings, microfilm and motion pictures

should be stored vertically and then periodically rewound to reduce the dangers of their sagging. Periodic inspection is also recommended. Where possible, a vault is recommended because it offers greater temperature/humidity control and safety from fire and other hazards. Other rare, fragile documents may also be kept in it.

Special Problems of Nitrate Film

Prior to World War II, nitrate-based photographic materials were rather common. They were produced in quantity for use in 35mm motion pictures and professional cut films. These films are particularly hazardous and should be kept away from all other archival materials. Duplicate copies should be made and the originals destroyed. In the past, many fires have been caused by the poor storage and handling of nitrate films. When stored in cans, as in the case of 35mm motion pictures, they tend to disintegrate into powder. In the process, an extremely hazardous fire potential is created. The film can literally explode. For this reason, nitrate-based films should be treated with great care and respect. While the heavier-weight nitrate cut films do not exhibit the same explosive qualities, they can be equally hazardous. Since they are usually kept in open files among other safety-base cut films, their deterioration is not always as apparent or dramatic. One should not be lulled by this because the deterioration is going on and in time the fumes and discoloration of the nitrate film can damage surrounding materials.

Unfortunately, identification of nitrate-based films is not always easy. In the past, edge markings have sometimes been incorporated. In recent years, safety base film has been regularly marked. Apparently there are still some foreign-made nitrate films which could appear in collections. One should be suspicious of any unmarked cut film or 35mm film whose manufacture predates 1952. There are some tests to indicate whether or not a film is nitrate. Burning is one of the quickest. If a piece of the film ignites quickly and rather spontaneously, it can usually be considered nitrate. Care should be taken when lighting the film as it can flame quickly.

Determining the pH of Paper

Whether a film is nitrate or not is an important aspect of film preservation; the same holds true in the determination of the pH of paper. While in many cases the visual evidence indicates that the paper is deteriorating (yellowing, fading of writing, etc.), the eye is not always able to distinguish the borderline cases and a test is needed to clarify them. For the uninitiated, pH is a scale of 1 to 10, designed to show the acidic or alkaline qualities of a paper, solution, chemical, etc. A pH of 7 is considered neutral, and the numbers below indicate acidic elements. Numbers above 7 show alkaline.

The methods used to determine pH are of two kinds, spot and meter tests. Spot tests are general in character and rely on a pH testing solution. In use, a drop of testing solution is placed on the paper and its color change evaluated. The more precise pH meter method requires sufficient equipment to make a determination. While very accurate, their utility to the average archives is limited.

The major problem the small, fledgling facility has in moving into the area of document repair is the lack of knowledge coupled with the lack of time. For instance, the deacidification of documents requires the physical setup and the staff time to man it. For the occasional user, it is usually not justifiable. A number of shops offer restoration services, such as: The Arbee Co., Inc., 6 Claremont Road, Bernardsville, N.J. 07924, and the W. J. Barrow Restoration Laboratory, Virginia Historical Society Building, 428 N. Blvd., Richmond, Va. 23221. These services can do much to help the infrequent user. State agencies in the Midwest and on the east and west coasts have in-house restoration services. Some of these shops do limited outside work for a fee. There is a movement now afoot to form regional centers for restoration work. The New England area has one in operation. There are also major facilities at the National Archives and the Library of Congress in Washington, D.C.

Conclusion

After one's archival house is in order, the serious archivist will undoubtedly wish to investigate the possibilities of employing some aspects of document restoration in his program. Depending on the needs of the collection, some repair methods may be employed. No matter what program is finally developed, the selected readings in the bibliography included in this issue will help the archivist to define his goals.

The User and the Used

Robert Rosenthal

Although there are abstract justifications for archival and manuscript collections, utility and the assumption of future use is basic
to their being. It boils down to that point when the user confronts
the repository and asks, "What is in it for me?" This meeting point
might be considered the crux of the enterprise. It is that time
when otherwise somnambulatory words and paper come alive to
revivify the past.

In the words that follow, I shall outline some of the assumptions
that lie immediately behind this point of contact, the rationale
behind some of the general procedural matters that take place. I
shall assume that the reader will consider himself equipped, however lightly, to apply the pertinency of these remarks to his own
circumstance. Alas, there is no formulary to prescribe the relationship which should exist between the user and the used. It has
psychological as well as intellectual currents running through it.
It is a managed situation, ostensibly formal in its relationships and
governed by rules, yet it is personal, as one individual becomes
dependent on the response of another.

One of the overriding conditions faced when broadly considering
use is the highly idiosyncratic character of both the institutions
and the users who wish to have access to them. Each institution is
"peculiar," although all may follow certain generally accepted
practices. If each institution has a certain genius, then each user
is especially endowed, coming to the institution with a problem
with a uniqueness all its own. As institutions may share practices,
users may be roughly classed by one means or another, but they
too remain inevitably different from one another. Appraising
these differences and reacting to them discriminatingly and fairly
is at the heart of any view of use and the user.

The curator (or whatever title the person may have who makes
substantive contact with the user) must be both judicious and
pragmatic in modulating the institutional response to the apparent requirements of the user. In order to respond properly there is

an assumption that the curator is knowledgeable about his
institution's holdings and is able to interpret them effectively.
Deeper still is the assumption that there is a desire and a willingness of the institution and its staff to respond. One might view this
contact with the user as a meeting of minds, but it is often minds
working at different levels and with differing points of view or
contexts. The exchange which takes place between the user and
the institution should be lucid, candid and decorous, for if it is
otherwise, the transfer of information can be distorted and mis-
apprehended.

With this introductory view stated, and before taking a closer view
of the process of engagement with the user, it might well be asked
who among a staff should have responsibility for this contact?
Ordinarily this would be called reference service. In large organizations with a strong functional deployment of staff, reference
departments are found with staff specifically assigned to respond
to users. They also have the responsibility of making referrals to
staff specialists, but normally they handle those queries within
their competency and also respond to special service requests,
such as photoreproduction, which come from users. Such a department would handle the broad orientation to the institution's
resources, as well as refer the user to special guides to the resources.

But many archival and manuscript collections are modest in size
or are so organized that an individual member of the staff carries
on a variety of functions, including service to the user. Whatever
the organization, the user should have a clear channel to the
appropriate member of the staff who is in the best position to be
of assistance. It is incumbent on the organization to create this
channel, for many, if not most, users enter a depository unaware
of how to obtain the most effective response to their needs. In
small, intimate depositories the problem is diminished but it can
become a source of concern as departments increase in size and
responsibilities proliferate.

Enter the User

As suggested above there is no typical user. While there may be
grounds for disputing this statement, the user himself does not
necessarily identify with other users. Although he may feel it pre-
sumptuous to think of himself unique in absolute terms, he prob-

The User and the Used

ably thinks of himself and his need for information as somehow different. In the face of this diversity, what can the institution rightfully assume about the user?

At a most basic level it can be assumed that the potential user of an archival or manuscript collection has a purpose for using such resources. Normally the use of manuscripts and archives is part of a serious inquiry, whether it be called research, now practically a catchword, or a healthy curiosity into some past phenomena. While there are degrees of research as well as degrees of curiosity, it is difficult for the curator to evaluate them except for the most blatant type of muckraking the record. And even in this latter instance, which comes infrequently enough, it is probably improper to inhibit access unless it falls clearly, and legally, outside the stated policies of the institution. The point here is that it is difficult, perhaps impossible, perhaps unwise, for the curator to delve too deeply into the motives and abilities of the potential user, so long as that user gives indications that he will abide by the institution's rules and regulations. Most depositories state or assume that to gain access to their holdings the user must be involved in bona fide activity, and it is doubted that any potential user would deny this. Thus the relationship between the user and the institution is largely based on good faith, faith on the part of the institution that the user states his purposes honestly and faith on the part of the user that the institution will respond to his need to the best of its ability.

There is another assumption we might have about this idiosyncratic user: that he comes with some prior knowledge of his subject and he has some reasonable degree of familiarity with what are known as the "secondary sources." That is, he has prepared himself for work with primary sources by first considering what others have written about the subject he is pursuing. This is not necessarily a valid criterion for access, but at least it can become a simple test that the curator can apply to the competency of the potential user. In the face of ignorance, the curator often turns tutor and, if tactfully presented, his knowledge of the subject (assuming he has it to offer) not only directly benefits the would-be user, but places the use of the primary sources in its proper perspective. But this assumption is a delicate one and must be handled accordingly.

The adjustment of the user to the material is frequently confounded by another barrier and the curator plays a crucial role in overcoming it. Although similar terminology is employed by both libraries and archives, different methodologies are at the root of each type of institution. Confusion over terminology can easily create misunderstanding about the user's approach to the material. If he is unfamiliar with the techniques or arrangement and description as applied to archives and manuscripts, he may initially conceive of his search in terms of classification and cataloging as normally applied to books. He may look for a classification of the material or a subject key to the material when none exists. In such instances, the curator must offer the user the rationale for the arrangement if it is not clearly stated in the descriptive guide or finding aid.

Thus we have entering the institution the sophisticated and the naive; the practiced researcher and the neophyte; those who are easily satisfied and those who may never be; those who express their needs simply and those who view their needs with complexity. Indeed, the curator does not know exactly what to expect until he has come in direct contact with the user. It is incumbent upon the curator to bring the user into the orbit of the institution's procedures and regulations as well as its special interpretive apparatus, and at the same time, to respect the integrity of the user's stated need. Accommodating the user can place a heavy and nettlesome burden on the curator. He must use his judgment, perhaps in areas where he has no firm knowledge, and he must develop his authority vis-a-vis the user, without inhibiting legitimate use. It is important for the curator to realize that he wields considerable power which will determine the success of the user's effort.

Arriving at Common Ground

Contact with the user is normally made in two ways, by personal contact upon the arrival of the user at the depository or by correspondence. Each type of contact requires a different approach; the former tends to be spontaneous and the latter more deliberate and protracted. With the individual at hand, the whole mechanism of service is usually put in motion without delay. The remote character of the exchange of information and service through correspondence is less susceptible to pressure and can be adjusted to other demands which may be faced by the staff. But it also means that more staff time is taken, since it can be assumed that, with the user present, he would be able to conduct his own search through guides, registers, or whatever other descriptive devices may be pertinent to his need. In the absence of the user, the staff must initiate the search and convey the information to the user. The degree to which the search is pursued will be discussed below.

The interview with the prospective user launches him into the workings of the depository. Since it is the first personal contact, its tone as well as its substance is important. It sets the stage for all future contact and should be handled with adroitness and understanding. It can determine the behavior of the user and his efficient use of his own time as well as that of the staff. If possible it should be held in privacy or semi-privacy, at least removed from constant interruption.

Four important matters should transpire at the interview: 1) the prospective user presents his credentials and delineates his problem, 2) he is introduced to the rules and regulations of the depository, 3) he is informed of the pertinent guides and services available to him, and 4) he is informed or introduced to other staff who may be able to assist him.

The prospective user's credentials should be presented early. This may be more a precaution than anything else, and normally the user will be happy to comply with such a request. The form of the credentials and an assessment of their value to the proceedings is a matter of judgment. More than anything else they establish the identity of the user and perhaps give some evidence of his competency. It is impossible to expect a uniform level in the credentials offered, although an attempt may be made to impose this. For example, a driver's license or institutional identification card may be asked for, or in the case of graduate students, a letter of introduction from faculty advisers may be required. Beyond establishing identity, however, such credentials can give little or no hint of a person's possible behavior.

Some users will come to the interview with a precise understanding of their problem and how it applies to the institution's resources. They have done their homework accurately and may be familiar with the guides to the records they wish to consult. In such instances, this part of the interview, when the purpose of access is discussed, may be perfunctory and skipped for all practical purposes.

But for many users the interview will be the first exposure to the institution. Both skill and knowledge is required by the interviewer to establish the prospective user's own understanding of his problem or query and to match his expectations with the institution's potential for response. Relying heavily on the user's prior knowledge of his subject, the two develop the tactics which should come into play in approaching a collection or a body of collections. The prospective user should come away from this encounter with some anticipation of the time and effort that will be required to probe the pertinent material, and the curator, with some assurance that the user understands how the material should be manipulated. Since this portion of the interview is essentially an exchange of relative expertise, it is important that the curator not dominate the meeting. In fact, he should rely heavily on the prior knowledge of the user, and weigh and counter this knowledge as it applies to the material in his custody. It often happens that this portion of the interview is transformed into an ongoing discussion after the user has begun to work through the records. This sustained relationship with the user may be of unusual benefit to the curator since it can reveal aspects of the material that have not been described in the finding aid apparatus. The user also stands to benefit from this exchange since it may afford the opportunity for the curator to bring newly pertinent resources to the user's attention. When this kind of relationship occurs it can be mutually rewarding.

The importance of the depository's rules and regulations are manifest, yet they require formal transmittal to the user. This can be done orally or in the form of printed directives, the former usually reinforcing and interpreting the latter. The rules usually cover behavior in the reading room, procedures for handling the material, literary rights and publication procedures, and so forth. The extent of detailed rules will depend on the size and traffic of the depository, but it is important that such rules are codified in order to apply them uniformly to all users. Such rules may be separately printed or incorporated in the application form which the user is required to submit. Obviously, such rules should be in the hands of the user before he commences his inspection of the material.

As the prospective user describes his problem, the curator's usual tactic is to respond with the description and location of the appropriate guide or finding aid. The extent to which the curator may wish to go into such matters will have to depend on his own assessment of the problem. It can be simple and direct or it could

The User and the Used

be involved, depending on the peculiarities of the guides and the character of the material. If material relevant to the user's need is restricted or otherwise unavailable for public access, it is incumbent on the curator to inform the prospective user of its existence, and at the same time, to explain the reasons and conditions governing nonavailability. This, it seems, is obligatory. The adjudication of any question concerning access to such material is left to the proper authority within the institution. It goes without saying that any properly imposed restrictions should be strictly adhered to unless countermanded by the appropriate authority.

Each institution will have its own procedures for putting the user in touch with its auxiliary services, such as photoreproduction. Again it is important for the user to be informed of both services and procedures from the beginning of work. This usually requires the transmittal of price schedules and the necessary forms to complete the process accurately. Providing reproductions of material may also lead to further explanation of the user's obligations regarding eventual use of the copies. The actual details and how they are spelled out will depend on each institution's policies.

The process of initiating the user may involve more than one member of the institutional staff. As the need for these other members of the staff is anticipated, they should be identified and introduced to the user. This not only adds to the comprehensiveness of the response, but allows the user to adjust his own strategy to what might be a complex search.

The correspondence which an institution receives concerning its resources will be equally varied. The lack of direct contact places a special burden on the curator, for unless the inquiry is specific, it will require some degree of interpretation. Writers of such correspondence often assume too much or too little and the common understanding that is usually achieved in the interview must be worked out through the exchange of letters.

The character or tone of the institutional side of the correspondence is as important as that suggested by the curator during the interview. It should be articulate and should convey to the writer a sense of the institution. The writer should be assured that the institution understands his inquiry and is in command of its response, that is, that it has properly applied the query to the institution's resources and policies. Unfortunately, many inquiries are neither specific nor well-stated. In such instances, a round of correspondence is required until a reasonable response can be made.

In the course of the correspondence, the basic elements which transpire during the interview must also be conveyed to the writer. The writer usually identifies himself in his letter and this may be substantiated by the letterhead. Certain aspects of the interview may be avoided, such as a description of the pertinent guides, since recourse to them is assumed by staff. In some instances a finding aid may be sent to the correspondent so he can make the selection of the appropriate material. But the most vexing aspect of the exchange of information by correspondence is the degree to which the institution will assume responsibility for the search for pertinent material, especially where large masses of material are concerned or the existing finding aids are not keyed to pinpointing the inquirer's problem, at least as he states it. This is an area requiring sensitive evaluation of the appropriateness of the institutional response. In some cases, the nature of the search may be clearly beyond institutional responsibility and the inquirer must personally attend to it himself. The exchange of correspondence may narrow the scope of the required search and allow the institution to attempt to make substantive response. How ever such issues are handled, they demand a special exercise of judgment that befits both the user and the institution.

Maintaining the Records of Use

The use of an institution's resources will generate certain documents which have special, if not permanent, value. If a user appears in person, he may be required to sign a register which records the time of his presence in the depository. He may also have to secure an identification or admission card, depending on what the institutional procedures are for visitors. But the basic document is the application form; it records the details of the user's identity, the material which he proposes to and will, in fact, use, and the purpose of this use. With the user's signature affixed, it also becomes an agreement with the institution, signifying that the user understands and will abide by the institution's policies and regulations. It has the effect of apprising the user of his obligations and establishing the record of use. Other information can be included on the application form as an institution deems necessary; for example, it may become the "call slip" for securing material from the stacks, depending on how it is devised. In any case it should become part of the institution's permanent record.

Another type of record which is usually created is for material processed for photoreproduction, again an important one for specifying exactly what material has been made available to the user. In the case of the application form and the photoreproduction order, it may be wise to see that the user receives a copy of the completed forms so he is fully aware of his part of the transaction. It is a simple way of avoiding confusion and misunderstanding. The institution may also find it necessary to maintain an internal register of the time during which particular material is being used in its reading room and is in the physical possession of the user. Beyond these records, others may be developed, but like all such records, they should be simply presented and their purpose manifest.

The maintenance of such records also serves various subsidiary purposes. They facilitate the internal manipulation of the material and permit constant control as they are handled by various staff and departments. They, together with whatever correspondence takes place, also have informational value about the use of particular material which can be passed on to other users. Placing such information in the hands of prospective users can be an important function of the curator; it is one way of avoiding unnecessary duplication of effort by users and assists in creating a network of individuals pursuing similar lines of inquiry.

It is one of the ironies of archival and manuscript depositories —although hardly unique to them—that they have swelled in size and have become efficient bureaucracies. This has tended to place the user in a relatively confined part of the enterprise although he is hardly forgotten. Along with this tendency is perhaps an unconscious attempt to over-anticipate, to stereotype, and otherwise process him through the institutional mysteries. In doing so, institutions, especially those charged with protecting and offering up the past, can lose their essential humaneness. The contact with the user is a special and continuous expression (and test) of the institution's character and sense of itself. If these matters are prized, then the user has a special place in our scheme of things.

Administering Archives and Manuscripts: A Selected Bibliography

Frank B. Evans

General Bibliographic Aids

The most useful guide to writings for the period before 1942 on administering archives and manuscripts is National Archives, *Selected Reference on Phases of Archival Administration,* compiled by Solon J. Buck and Ernst Posner, Staff Information Circulars, no. 12 (Washington: National Archives, 1942). In addition to many annotated entries it includes the most influential European writings to that date. For the period since 1942, the most comprehensive guide is the annual series of classified bibliographies published in the *American Archivist* beginning in 1943, most recently under the title, "Writings on Archives, Current Records, and Historical Manuscripts."

A convenient classified and subject-indexed compilation of these writings, supplemented from other sources, is National Archives and Records Service, *The Administration of Modern Archives: A Select Bibliographic Guide,* compiled by Frank B. Evans (Washington: National Archives and Records Service, 1970). An expanded and revised second edition is scheduled for publication by the Society of American Archivists. Also useful on particular topics is Frederick L. Rath, Jr., and Marilyn R. O'Connell, comps., *Guide to Historic Preservation, Historical Agencies, and Museum Practices: A Selective Bibliography,* 2d rev. ed. (Cooperstown: American Association for State and Local History, 1970).

General Works and Manuals

On public archives, the most basic and influential works have been two treaties by Theodore R. Schellenberg, *Modern Archives: Principles and Techniques* (Chicago: University of Chicago Press, 1956), hereafter cited as Schellenberg, *Modern Archives;* and *The Management of Archives* (New York: Columbia University Press, 1965), hereafter cited as Schellenberg, *Management of Archives.*

A Selected Bibliography

Ernst Posner, *American State Archives* (Chicago: University of Chicago Press, 1964), hereafter cited as Posner, *State Archives,* goes beyond its title in the analysis of archival functions and is particularly valuable for the standards it has established.

On personal papers and manuscripts, the most useful manuals are Ruth B. Bordin and Robert M. Warner, *The Modern Manuscript Library* (Metuchen: Scarecrow Press, 1966), hereafter cited as Bordin and Warner, *Manuscript Library;* and Lucile M. Kane, *A Guide to the Care and Administration of Manuscripts,* 2d ed. (Nashville: American Association for State and Local History, 1966), hereafter cited as Kane, *Manuscripts.* A new manual covering both archives and manuscripts is being prepared for the American Association for State and Local History by Kenneth W. Duckett. See also Maynard J. Brichford et al., *Proceedings of the Conference on Archival Administration for Small Universities, Colleges, and Junior Colleges,* University of Illinois Graduate School of Library Science, Occasional Paper No. 88 (Urbana: 1967).

More selective in their coverage but also valuable are Philip C. Brooks, *Research in Archives: The Use of Unpublished Primary Sources* (Chicago: University of Chicago Press, 1969), hereafter cited as Brooks, *Research in Archives;* and many of the essays in William B. Hasseltine and Donald R. McNeil, eds., *In Support of Clio: Essays in Memory of Herbert A. Kellar* (Madison: State Historical Society of Wisconsin, 1958); essays in Kenneth W. Munden, ed., *Archives and the Public Interest: Selected Essays by Ernst Posner* (Washington: Public Affairs Press, 1967); and those in Rolland E. Stevens, ed., *University Archives: Papers Presented at an Institute Conducted by the University of Illinois Graduate School of Library Science, November 1-4, 1964* (Champaign: University of Illinois, 1965), hereafter cited as Stevens, *University Archives.* Still useful for background, rather than for current policies and practices, is R. G. W. Vail, issue ed., "Manuscripts and Archives," *Library Trends* 5 (no. 3, January 1957), entire issue. A very convenient summary of the literature to about 1966 on the origin and development of archival agencies and manuscript repositories, public and private, is O. Lawrence Burnette, Jr., *Beneath the Footnote: A Guide to the Use and Preservation of American Historical Sources* (Madison: State Historical Society of Wisconsin, 1969), hereafter cited as Burnette, *Beneath the Footnote.*

A Selected Bibliography

Terminology and Principles

Particularly useful are Brooks, *Research in Archives,* pp. 1-13; Robert L. Brubaker, "Archival Principles and the Curator of Manuscripts," *American Archivist* 29 (October 1966): 505-514; Lester J. Cappon, "Historical Manuscripts as Archives: Some Definitions and Their Application," *American Archivist* 19 (April 1956): 101-110; Frank B. Evans, "Modern Concepts of Archives Administration and Records Management," *Unesco Bulletin for Libraries* 24 (September-October 1970): 242-247; Oliver W. Holmes, "History and Theory of Archival Practice," in Stevens, *University Archives,* pp. 1-21; and Schellenberg, *Modern Archives,* pp. 11-16. See especially Society of American Archivists, Committee on Terminology, *A Glossary of Basic Terms for Archivists, Manuscript Curators, and Records Managers,* compiled by Frank B. Evans, Donald F. Harrison, and Edwin A. Thompson, edited by William L. Rofes (Ann Arbor: Society of American Archivists, 1973), a revision of which will be published in the July 1974 issue of the *American Archivist.*

On public records and archives see also Oliver Holmes, " 'Public Records'—Who Knows What They Are?" *American Archivist* 23 (January 1960): 3-26; National Archives, *Archival Principles: Selections from the Writings of Waldo Gifford Leland,* Staff Information Papers, no. 20 (Washington: National Archives and Records Service, 1955); and Margaret C. Norton, "Some Legal Aspects of Archives," *American Archivist* 8 (January 1945): 1-11.

Archivists and Librarians

Similarities and differences are explored in Robert H. Bahmer, "Archives," in Allen Kent and Harold Lancour, eds., *Encyclopedia of Library and Information Services,* vol. 1 (New York: Marcel Dekker, Inc., 1968-   ), pp. 515-519; Philip C. Brooks, "Archivists and Their Colleagues: Common Denominators," *American Archivist* 14 (January 1951): 33-45; Moreau B. C. Chambers, "The Librarian as Archivist," *Catholic Library World* 45 (February 1974): 326-329; Randolph W. Church, "The Relationship Between Archival Agencies and Libraries," *American Archivist* 6 (July 1943): 145-150; Verner W. Clapp, "Archivists and Bibliographical Control: A Librarian's Viewpoint," *American Archivist* 14 (October 1951): 305-311; Herman Kahn, "Librarians and Archivists—Some Aspects of Their Partnership," *American Archivist* 7 (October 1944): 243-251; L. Quincy Mumford, "Archivists and Librarians:

A Selected Bibliography

Time for a New Look," *American Archivist* 33 (July 1970): 269-274; Margaret C. Norton, "Archives and Libraries: A Comparison Drawn," in Illinois, Secretary of State, *Bluebook, 1939-1940,* pp. 427-443; Posner, *State Archives,* pp. 345-347, 357-358; Schellenberg, *Management of Archives,* pp. 20-31, 119-143; and Schellenberg, *Modern Archives,* pp. 17-25.

For comparative purposes see also Philip Hepworth, "Manuscripts and Non-Book Material in Libraries," *Archives* 9 (October 1969): 90-97; J. D. Hine, "How Librarians Need Archivists," *Archives and Manuscripts* 5 (November 1972): 14-17; Library Association, "The Place of Archives and Manuscripts in the Field of Librarianship," *Library Association Record* 71 (January 1969): 15, reprinted in *Archives* 9 (April 1969): 40-41, and in *Society of Archivists Journal* 3 (October 1969): 582-583; Philip Monypenny, *The Library Function of the States: Commentary on the Survey of Library Functions of the States* (Chicago: American Library Association, 1966), pp. 121-128; and Armando Petrucci, "Archives and Libraries: Possibilities of Collaboration," *Unesco Bulletin for Libraries* 50 (March-April 1966): 65-70.

Establishing a Program

Suggestive of administrative considerations and various approaches are Robert H. Bahmer, "The Management of Archival Institutions," *American Archivist* 26 (January 1963): 3-10; Maynard J. Brichford, "Informing the Government About Its Archives," *American Archivist* 30 (October 1967): 565-573; Henry J. Browne, "An Appeal for Archives in Institutions of Higher Learning," *American Archivist* 16 (July 1953): 213-226; Browne, "A Plan of Organization for a University Archives," *American Archivist* 12 (October 1949): 355-358; Miriam I. Crawford, "Interpreting the University Archives to the Librarian," *Pennsylvania Library Association Bulletin* 23 (November 1968): 349-358; Helen L. Davidson, "Selling Management on Business Archives," *Records Management Quarterly* 3 (July 1969): 15-19; David B. Gracy, II, "Starting an Archives," *Georgia Archive* 1 (Fall 1972): 20-29; Posner, *State Archives,* pp. 308-318, 349-367; Schellenberg, *Modern Archives,* pp. 117-132; and Woodrow W. Wasson, "Organizing and Administering a University Archives," *College & Research Libraries* 29 (March 1968): 109-116.

Also suggestive of responsibilities, functions and organizational relationships, even for small, private repositories, are the following reports of various committees of the Society of American Archivists: "The Proposed Uniform State Public Records Act," *American Archivist* 3 (April 1940): 107-115; "A Proposed Model Act to Create a State Department of Archives and History," *American Archivist* 7 (April 1940): 130-133; and "A Model Bill for a State Archives Department," *American Archivist* 10 (January 1947): 47-49.

On education and training for archival work, the most recent summary is Robert M. Warner, "Archival Training in the United States and Canada," *American Archivist* 35 (July-October 1972): 347-358.

Use of Archives and Manuscripts

On this topic there is a wide range of writings. Among the most valuable are Bordin and Warner, *Manuscript Library,* pp. 69-78, 101-121; Brooks, *Research in Archives,* pp. 36-73; Frank B. Evans, "The State Archivist and the Academic Researcher—'Stable Companionship,' " *American Archivist* 26 (July 1963): 319-321; Philip D. Jordan, "The Scholar and the Archivist—A Partnership," *American Archivist* 31 (January 1968): 57-65; John A. Munroe, "A Brave Man—or a Foolish One," *American Archivist* 26 (April 1963): 151-160; Wyman W. Parker, "How Can the Archivist Aid the Researcher?" *American Archivist* 16 (July 1953): 233-240; Howard H. Peckham, "Aiding the Scholar in Using Manuscript Collections," *American Archivist* 19 (July 1956): 221-228; Jean Preston, "Problems in the Use of Manuscripts," *American Archivist* 28 (July 1965): 367-379; Walter Rundell, Jr., "Relations Between Historical Researchers and Custodians of Source Materials," *College & Research Libraries* 29 (November 1968): 466-476; and Schellenberg, *Modern Archives,* pp. 224-236.

See also "The Archivist's Code," *American Archivist* 18 (October 1955): 307-308; W. Kaye Lamb, "The Archivist and the Historian," *American Historical Review* 68 (January 1963): 385-391; A. M. Patterson, "State Archival Agencies' Services to Other State Agencies," *American Historical Review* 26 (July 1963): 315-318; Kenneth W. Richards, "The State Archivist and the Amateur Researcher," *American Historical Review* 26 (July 1963): 323-326; Albert B. Rollins, Jr., "The Historian and the Archivist," *American Historical Review* 32 (October 1969): 369-374; Milton Rubicam, "What the Genealogist Expects of an Archival Agency or Historical Society," *American Historical Review* 12 (October 1949):

A Selected Bibliography

333-338; and Walter Rundell, Jr., *In Pursuit of American History: Research and Training in the United States* (Norman: University of Oklahoma Press, 1970), pp. 3-36, 284-334.

Collecting Manuscripts

On the historical background, see Richard D. Altick, *The Scholar Adventurers* (New York: A. A. Knopf, 1963), pp. 86-121; Robert G. Ballantine, "Records and Archives of the Professions," *American Archivist* 29 (April 1966): 187-195; Robert L. Brubaker, "Manuscript Collections," *Library Trends* 13 (October 1964): 226-253; Burnette, *Beneath the Footnote,* pp. 135-264; Robert W. Hill, "Literary, Artistic, and Musical Manuscripts," *Library Trends* 5 (January 1957): 322-329; Lucile M. Kane, "Manuscript Collecting, in William B. Hesseltine and Donald R. McNeil, eds., *In Support of Clio: Essays in Memory of Herbert A. Kellar* (Madison: State Historical Society of Wisconsin, 1958), pp. 29-48; and David C. Mearns, "Historical Manuscripts, Including Personal Papers," *Library Trends* 5 (January 1957): 313-321.

On problems and techniques involved in developing an effective acquisition program, see particularly Paul M. Angle, "The University Library and Its Manuscripts: An Excursion Into Other People's Business," *Library Quarterly* 15 (April 1945): 123-130; Bordin and Warner, *Manuscript Library,* pp. 9-38; Richard C. Berner, "On Ephemera: Their Collection and Use," *Library Resources & Technical Services* 7 (Fall 1963): 335-339; Maynard J. Brichford, "University Archives: Relationships with Faculty," *American Archivist* 34 (April 1971): 173-181; "Collecting Policies," in Laurence J. Kipp, ed., *Source Materials for Business and Economic History* (Cambridge: Harvard Graduate School of Business Administration, 1967), pp. 9-39; Robert B. Downs, "Collecting Manuscripts: By Libraries," *Library Trends* 5 (January 1957): 337-343; David C. Duniway, "Conflicts in Collecting," *American Archivist* 24 (January 1961): 55-63; Duniway, "Where Do Public Records Belong?" *American Archivist* 31 (January 1968): 49-55; A. Hunter Dupree, "What Manuscripts the Historian Wants Saved," *Isis* 53 (March 1962): 62-66.

Harley P. Holden, "Collecting of Faculty Papers," *Harvard Library Bulletin* 19 (April 1971): 187-193; Barbara J. Kaiser, "Problems with Donors of Contemporary Collections," *American Archivist* 32 (April 1969): 103-107; Thomas K. Krasean, "Impressions of a Field Representative in Search of Historical Manuscripts," *Library*

Occurrent 23 (November 1969): 123-124; Paul Lewinson, "Archival Sampling," *American Archivist* 20 (October 1957): 291-312; Lewinson, "Toward Accessioning Standards—Research Records," *American Archivist* 23 (July 1960): 297-309; Richard B. Sealock, "Acquisition and Organization of Local History Materials in Libraries," *Library Trends* 13 (October 1969): 179-191; and "Where are the Historical Manuscripts? A Symposium," *American Association for State and Local History Bulletin* 2 (September 1950): 103-127.

Arrangement and Description

On the application of archival principles of arrangement and of the techniques of collective description see: Richard C. Berner, "Manuscript Collections and Archives—A Unitary Approach," *Library Resources & Technical Services* 9 (Spring 1965): 213-220; Bordin and Warner, *Manuscript Library,* pp. 50-68; Katherine E. Brand, "The Place of the Register in the Manuscript Division of the Library of Congress," *American Archivist* 18 (January 1955): 59-67; Frank B. Evans, "Modern Methods of Arrangement of Archives in the United States," *American Archivist* 29 (April 1966): 241-263; Robert S. Gordon, "Suggestions for Organization and Description of Archival Holdings of Local Historical Societies," *American Archivist* 26 (January 1963): 19-39; Oliver W. Holmes, "Archival Arrangement—Five Different Operations at Five Different Levels," *American Archivist* 27 (January 1964): 21-41; Kane, *Manuscripts,* pp. 51-63.

Dorothy V. Martin, "Use of Cataloging Techniques in Work with Records and Manuscripts," *American Archivist* 18 (October 1955): 317-336; National Archives, *The Control of Records at the Record Group Level,* Staff Information Circulars, no. 16 (Washington: National Archives and Records Service, 1950); National Archives, *The Preparation of Lists of Record Items,* Staff Information Papers, no. 17, rev. (Washington: National Archives and Records Service, 1950); National Archives, *Principles of Arrangement,* Staff Information Papers, no. 18 (Washington: National Archives and Records Service, 1951); Amy W. Nyholm, "Modern Manuscripts: A Functional Approach," *Library Resources & Technical Services* 14 (Summer 1970): 325-340; Schellenberg, *Management of Archives,* pp. 32-198, 219-301; Schellenberg, *Modern Archives,* pp. 168-214.

On the use of automated techniques, see especially Frank B. Burke, "The Application of Automated Techniques in the Man-

A Selected Bibliography

agement and Control of Source Material," *American Archivist* 30 (April 1967): 255-278, and other articles in this same issue, and Burke, "The Impact of the Specialist on Archives," *College & Research Libraries* 33 (July 1972): 312-317.

Legal Problems

Many of the writings listed above under the heading Use of Archives and Manuscripts deal in general with problems of access, literary property and copyrights. See also Bordin and Warner, *Manuscript Library,* pp. 69-78, 101-121; Brooks, *Research in Archives,* pp. 49-73; Melville Cane, "Who Owns Your Letters? The Paper Belongs to You, But Not the Message," *Autograph Collectors Journal* 2 (April 1950): 19-22; Verner W. Clapp, "The Copyright Dilemma: A Librarian's View,"*Library Quarterly* 38 (October 1968): 352-387; Seymour V. Connor, "The Problem of Literary Property in Archival Depositories," *American Archivist* 21 (April 1958): 143-152; Henry Bartholomew Cox, "The Impact of the Proposed Copyright Law Upon Scholars and Custodians," *American Archivist* 29 (April 1966): 217-227; Cox, "Private Letters and the Public Domain," *American Archivist* 28 (July 1965): 381-388.

Julius J. Marke, "Copyright and Intellectual Property," *Albany Law Review* 32 (Fall 1967): 1-57; Walter Rundell, Jr., "The Recent American Past v. *HR* 4347: Historian's Dilemma," *American Archivist* 29 (April 1966): 209-215; Ralph R. Shaw, *Literary Property in the United States* (Metuchen: Scarecrow Press, 1950); Louis C. Smith, "The Copying of Literary Property in Library Collections," *Law Library Journal* 46 (August 1953): 197-206, and 47 (August 1954): 204-208; and Kenneth E. Waldren, "Common Law Right in Literary Property," *Patent Office Society Journal* 37 (September 1955): 642-659.

See also Association of College and Research Libraries, Committee on the Use of Manuscripts by Visiting Scholars, "Report," *College & Research Libraries* 13 (January 1952): 58-60; Edgar R. Harlan, "Ethics Involved in the Handling of Personal Papers," *Annals of Iowa,* 3d series, 16 (April 1929): 610-621; Mark L. Ireland, "The Right of Privacy as it Affects History and Genealogy," *Michigan History* 35 (June 1951): 202-206; Walter Rundell, Jr., "Restricted Records: Suggestions From the Survey," *AHA Newsletter* 7 (June 1969): 39-43; and Noel C. Stevenson, "Genealogy and the Right of Privacy," *American Genealogist* 25 (July 1949): 145-152.

A Selected Bibliography

Nontextual Material

On maps, charts and related cartographic archives, see Ralph E. Ehrenberg, "Map Acquisition, Arrangement, and Description at the National Archives," Special Libraries Association, *Geography and Map Division Bulletin* 68 (June 1967): 10-13; and Schellenberg, *Management of Archives,* pp. 302-321.

On still picture and other pictorial records, see Schellenberg, *Management of Archives,* pp. 322-343; Renata V. Shaw, "Picture Organization Practices and Procedures, Part I," *Special Libraries* 63 (October 1972): 448-456, and "Part II," *Special Libraries* 63 (November 1972): 502-506; Shaw, "Picture Searching, 1. Techniques," *Special Libraries* 62 (December 1971): 524-528, and "2. Tools," *Special Libraries* 63 (January 1972): 13-24; Paul Vanderbilt, "Filing Your Photographs: Some Basic Procedures," American Association for State and Local History, Technical Leaflet, no. 36, in *History News* 21 (June 1966): 117-124. See also Waldo H. Moore, "Copyright of Pictorial Material," *Special Libraries* 56 (January 1956): 20-22.

On motion pictures, see Hermine M. Baumhofer, "Film Records Management," *American Archivist* 19 (July 1956): 235-248; John G. Bradley, "Cataloguing and Indexing Motion Picture Film," *American Archivist* 81 (July 1945): 169-184; Barrie E. King, "Film Archives: Their Purpose and Problems," *Archives and Manuscripts* 4 (May 1970): 8-16; and John B. Kuiper, "The Historical Value of Motion Pictures," *American Archivist* 31 (October 1968): 385-390. Useful on sound recordings are Edward E. Colby, "Sound Scholarship: Scope, Purpose, Function, and Potential of Phonorecord Archives," *Library Trends* 21 (July 1972): 7-28; and James D. Porter, "Sound in the Archives," in "Technical Notes," *American Archivist* 27 (April 1964): 327-336.

Preservation

Basic readings on storage equipment and facilities are Victor Gondos, Jr., ed., *Reader for Archives and Records Center Buildings* (Ann Arbor: Society of American Archivists, 1970); Virginia L. Mauck, "Selection and Purchase of Archival Equipment and Supplies," *Illinois Libraries* 53 (January 1971): 18-22; Harold E. Nelson, "Fire Protection for Archives and Records Centers," *Records Management Quarterly* 2 (January 1968): 19-23; Schel-

A Selected Bibliography

lenberg, *Management of Archives,* pp. 199-218; and Schellenberg, *Modern Archives,* pp. 161-164.

On repair and restoration, see Robert H. Bahmer, "Recent American Developments in Archival Repair, Preservation, and Photo-
graphy," *Archivum* 10 (1960): 59-71; George M. Cunha and
Dorothy G. Cunha, *Conservation of Library Materials: A Manual
and Bibliography on the Care, Repair, and Restoration of Library
Materials,* 2d ed., 2 vols. (Metuchen: Scarecrow Press, 1971); National Archives, *The Rehabilitation of Paper Records,* Staff Information Papers, no. 16 (Washington: National Archives and Records Service, 1950); National Archives, *The Repair and Preservation of Records* by Adelaide E. Minogue, Bulletin No. 5 (Washington: National Archives, 1943); Frazer G. Poole, "Preservation
Costs and Standards," *Special Libraries* 59 (October 1968):
614-619; and Schellenberg, *Modern Archives,* pp. 164-167.

See also, on nontextual holdings, Robert I. Boak, "Restoration
and Preservation of Maps," Special Libraries Association,
Geography and Map Division Bulletin 81 (September 1970):
21-23; and Marie T. Capps, "Preservation and Maintenance of
Maps," *Special Libraries* 63 (October 1973): 457-462. On still pictures, see George T. Eaton, "Preservation, Deterioration, Restoration of Photographic Images," *Library Quarterly* 40 (January
1970): 85-98; and Eastman Kodak Company, *Filing Negatives and
Transparencies,* Kodak Pamphlet P-12 (Rochester: Eastman
Kodak Company, 1960).

For motion pictures, see John M. Calhoun, "The Preservation of
Motion-Picture Film,"*American Archivist* 30 (July 1967): 517-526;
and Francis W. Decker, "The Care of Motion Picture Film,"
American Archivist 25 (July 1962): 357-359. For magnetic tape,
see Harold E. Nelson, "Protection and Storage of EDP Tapes,"
Records Management Journal 4 (Winter 1966): 15-17; and Bruce
Shapley, "The Care and Storage of Magnetic Tape," *Data Proces-
sing Magazine* 10 (April 1968): 80-81.

On security, vandalism and thefts, see also Robert H. Land, "Defense of Archives against Human Foes," *American Archivist* 19
(April 1956): 121-138; James B. Rhoads, "Alienation and Thievery:
Archival Problems," *American Archivist* 29 (April 1966): 197-208;
and Matt Roberts, "Guards, Turnstiles, Electric Devices, and the
Illusion of Security," *College & Research Libraries* 29 (July 1968):
259-275.

Appendix: Terminology

Richard H. Lytle

The terminology of archives administration is chaotic. A recent effort to rationalize the situation is a glossary published in the *American Archivist* in July 1974.[1] All definitions quoted below are taken from the glossary and are reprinted here by permission of the Society of American Archivists.

First, a distinction must be attempted between *archives* and *manuscripts* or *manuscript collections:*

ARCHIVES. (1) The noncurrent records of an organization or institution preserved because of their continuing value; also referred to, in this sense, as archival materials or archival holdings. (2) The agency responsible for selecting, preserving, and making available archival materials; also referred to as an archival agency. (3) The building or part of a building where such materials are located; also referred to as an archival repository (or, in U.S. Govt., archival depository). In American usage, the term *archives* is generally a plural or collective noun, although the form *archive* has been applied to a number of special collections.

[MANUSCRIPT] COLLECTION. (1) An artificial accumulation of manuscripts or documents devoted to a single theme, person, event, or type of record. (2) A body of manuscripts or papers, including associated printed or near-print materials, having a common source. If formed by or around an individual or family, such materials are more properly termed *personal papers* or *records*. If the cumulation is that of a corporate entity, it is more properly termed *records*. (3) In singular or plural form, the total holdings—accessions and deposits—of a repository.

MANUSCRIPTS. Documents of manuscript character usually having historical or literary value or significance. All manuscript records may thus be regarded as manuscripts, but generally the term is used to distinguish nonarchival from archival material. Included in the term are bodies or groups of personal papers with organic unity, artificial collections of documents acquired from various sources usually according to a plan but without regard to provenance, and individual documents acquired by a manuscript repository because of their special importance.

Terminology

RECORDS. All recorded information, regardless of media or characteristics, made or received and maintained by an organization or institution in pursuance of its legal obligations or in the transaction of its business.

If an organization or institution—church or government agency, for example—maintains its own record in accordance with archival principles, the result is an archives. The papers of a poet are manuscripts, or a manuscript collection. But there is no precise division between archives and manuscripts so far as physical type and organization are concerned, in that many manuscript collections exhibit most characteristics of archival bodies and can be effectively administered by the techniques of archival administration.

The problem of making a consistent distinction between archives and manuscript collections must be kept in mind while reading the articles in this issue. Paul McCarthy's overview article deals with both institutional archival depositories and manuscript collections. Other authors use the terms interchangeably, or their comments refer equally to archives and manuscript collections.

Two terms important for archival principles are defined as follows:

FONDS. A term widely used in Europe to designate for control purposes the archives of a particular type of institution or organization; a term comparable to the concept of a record group.

PROVENANCE. (1) In general archival and manuscript usage, the "office of origin" of records, i.e., that office or administrative entity that created or received and accumulated the records in the conduct of its business. Also the person, family, firm, or other source of personal papers and manuscript collections. (2) Information of successive transfers of ownership and custody of a particular manuscript. (3) In archival theory, the principle that archives of a given record creator must not be intermingled with those of other records creators. The principle is frequently referred to by the French expression, *respect des fonds*. A corollary, frequently designated as a separate principle, is the Principle of Sanctity of the Original Order (or *respect pour l'ordre primitif, Registratur Prinzip,* or Registry Principle).

Note that Richard Berner, in the article on arrangement and description, makes some of the distinctions between terms referred to in these definitions.

Terminology

Some additional useful terms are:

ACCESSION. (1) The act and procedures involved in a transfer of legal title and the taking of records or papers into the physical custody of an archival agency, records center, or manuscript repository. In records center operations, transfer of legal title may not be involved. (2) The materials involved in such a transfer of custody.

ADMINISTRATIVE VALUE. In appraisal, the usefulness of records to the originating or succeeding agency in the conduct of current business. In nongovernment use, the phrase *operational value* is also used.

APPRAISAL. (1) The process of determining the value and thus the disposition of records based upon their current administrative, legal, and fiscal use; their evidential and informational or research value; their arrangement; and their relationship to other records. Sometimes referred to as selective retention. (2) The monetary evaluation of gifts of manuscripts.

ARCHIVAL INTEGRITY. The standard that requires that archival holdings be identified and arranged by provenance, maintained in their original filing order, and preserved in their entirety without mutilation, alteration, or unauthorized destruction of any part of them.

ARRANGEMENT. The process and results of organizing archives, records, and manuscripts in accordance with accepted archival principles, particularly provenance, at as many as necessary of the following levels: repository, record group or comparable control unit, subgroup(s), series, file unit, and document. The process usually includes packing, labeling, and shelving of archives, records, and manuscripts, and is intended to achieve physical or administrative control and basic identification of the holdings.

CALENDAR. A chronological list of individual documents, either selective or comprehensive, usually with a description giving one or more of the following: writer, recipient, date, place, summary of content, type of manuscript, and page or leaf count.

CLASSIFICATION. (1) The predesignated filing system for a record series. (2) The act of identifying documents or records in accordance with a predesignated filing system.

CORRESPONDENCE. Letters, postcards, memoranda, notes, telecommunications, and any other form of addressed, written communications sent and received.

DESCRIPTION. The process of establishing intellectual control over holdings through the preparation of finding aids.

DOCUMENT. (1) Recorded information regardless of medium or characteristics. Frequently used interchangeably with *record.* (2) A single record or manuscript item. When abbreviated, *D.* or *Doc.,* it designates any manuscript that is not a letter.

FINDING AIDS. The descriptive media, published and unpublished, created by an originating office, an archival agency, or manuscript repository, to establish physical or administrative and intellectual control over records and other holdings. Basic finding aids include guides (general or repository and subject or topical), inventories or registers, location registers, card catalogs, special lists, shelf and box lists, indexes, calendars, and, for machine-readable records, software documentation.

GUIDE. At the repository level, a finding aid that briefly describes and indicates the relationships between holdings, with record groups, papers, collections, or comparable bodies of material as the units of entry. Guides may also be limited to the description of the holdings of one or more repositories relating to particular subjects, periods, or geographical areas.

HOLOGRAPH. A document in the handwriting of the person who signs it. The term is used throughout to indicate that the entire document, not only the signature, is autograph.

INVENTORY. (1) A basic archival finding aid that generally includes a brief history of the organization and functions of the agency whose records are being described; a descriptive list of each record series giving as a minimum such data as title, inclusive dates, quantity, arrangement, relationships to other series, and description of significant subject content; and, if appropriate, appendices which provide such supplementary information as a glossary of abbreviations and special terms, lists of folder headings on special subjects, or selective indexes. (2) In records management the term is used to describe a survey of records prior to disposition or the development of records retention schedules.

ITEM. The smallest unit of record material which accumulates to form file units and series, e.g., a letter, memorandum, report, leaflet, photograph, or reel of film or tape.

MANUSCRIPT. A handwritten or typed document, including a letterpress or carbon copy. A mechanically produced form completed in handwriting or typescript is also considered a manuscript.

MANUSCRIPT GROUP. An organized body of related papers or a collection, comparable to a record group, for control purposes.

PAPERS. (1) A natural accumulation of personal and family materials, as distinct from records. (2) A general term used to designate more than one type of manuscript material.

PIECE. (1) A discrete object or individual member of a class or group, as a letter. In this sense, piece is synonymous with item or document. (2) A fragment or part separated from the whole in any manner, for example by cutting or detaching, as a separated leaf of a multipage document.

PROCESSING. The activities intended to facilitate the use of personal papers and manuscript collections generally comparable to arrangement, description, and preservation of archival material.

RECORD. (1) Recorded information regardless of media of characteristics. (2) In machine-readable records/archives, two or more data fields in predetermined order and treated as a unit.

RECORD GROUP. A body of organizationally related records established on the basis of provenance with particular regard for the administrative history, the complexity, and the volume of the records and archives of the institution or organization involved. Collective and general record groups represent modification of this basic concept for convenience in arrangement, description, and reference service.

REGISTER. (1) The list of events, letters sent and received, actions taken, etc., usually in simple sequence, as by date or number, and often serving as a finding aid to the records, such as a register of letters or a register of visitors. . . .

SERIES. File units or documents arranged in accordance with a filing system or maintained as a unit because they relate to a particular subject or function, result from the same activity, have a particular form, or because of some other relationship arising out of their creation, receipt, or use. Sometimes known as a *record series.*

SUBGROUP. A body of related records within a record group, usually consisting of the records of a primary subordinate administrative unit. Subgroups may also be established for related bodies of records within a record group that can best be delimited in terms of functional, geographical, or chronological relationships. Subgroups, in turn, are divided into as many levels as are necessary to reflect the successive organizational units that constitute the hierarchy of the subordinate administrative unit or that will assist in grouping series entries in terms of their relationships.

SUBSERIES. An aggregate of file units within a record series readily separable in terms of physical class, type, form, subject, or filing arrangement.

Terminology

The definitions above—especially those relating to record group, subgroup, series, and subseries—are made mostly in the context of large institutional archives. Some of the definitions vary from those of Richard Berner's in his article on arrangement and description, but his use of the terms is very helpful in adapting archival methodology to manuscript collections.

Notes

1 Frank B. Evans, Donald F. Harrison, and Edwin A. Thompson, comps., and William L. Rofes, ed., "A Basic Glossary for Archivists, Manuscript Curators, and Records Managers," *The American Archivist* 37 (no. 3, July 1974): 415-433.

Contributors

Richard C. Berner is head of the University Archives and Manuscripts Division of the University of Washington Libraries, and is University Archivist, holding this position since 1967. From 1958 to 1967 he was Curator of Manuscripts. He is on the Council of the Society of American Archivists (1972-76) and is a Fellow of the SAA.

Henry Bartholomew Cox is currently a student of law at the National Law Center of George Washington University. His doctorate in American Diplomatic History from George Washington University preceded eight years of service in the federal government, first in the Historical Office of the Department of State, and later at the National Archives and Records Service where his work included service as Assistant to the Executive Director of the National Historical Publications Commission and most recently, 1971-1973, as Director of the Center for the Documentary Study of the American Revolution.

Ralph E. Ehrenberg is a graduate of the University of Minnesota. He joined the staff of the National Archives in 1966 and is currently director of the Cartographic Archives Division. His article, "Non-Geographic Methods of Map Arrangement and Classification," appeared in the October 1973 issue of the *Drexel Library Quarterly.*

Frank B. Evans is Regional Commissioner for Region 3, National Archives and Records Service, General Services Administration, and Adjunct Professor in the Department of History of the American University, Washington, D. C. His PhD in history was received from the Pennsylvania State University, where from 1949 to 1958 he served on the faculty. From 1958 to 1963 he was Associate State Archivist and then State Archivist of Pennsylvania. He joined the National Archives and Record Service in 1963. He is active in a number of national and international historical and archival organizations and serves as the U.S. correspondent for *Archivum* and as editor of the foreign abstracts department of the *American Archivist.*

Richard H. Lytle is Archivist of the Smithsonian Institution, a position he has held since 1969. Prior to coming to the Smithsonian he was Archivist of Rice University (1968-1969), Archivist of Washington University (1964-1968) and Assistant Local Records Archivist of the State of Illinois (1963-1964). Mr. Lytle has served in several capacities in the Society of American Archivists, including the chairmanship of the committee on the

Contributors

archives of science. He has assisted in development of archives administration courses for librarians at Washington University, and has a continuing interest in the relationship between library science and archives administration. Presently he is pursuing a PhD program in the College of Library and Information Services, University of Maryland.

Paul H. McCarthy, Jr., has been Archivist and Curator of Manuscripts at the University of Alaska, Fairbanks, since 1965 and holds the rank of Associate Professor of Library Science. He holds a BA in History from St. John Fisher College, an MSLS from Syracuse University. In addition he holds a Certificate in Archival Administration from American University/ National Archives and has done graduate work in history. He has been a member of various professional committees in the Society of American Archivists, is a founding member, a member of the Board of Directors and past president of the Alaska Historical Society, and past president of the Alaska Library Association.

Mary Lynn McCree has been Curator of the restored Jane Addams' Hull House and Manuscript Librarian of the University of Illinois at Chicago since 1966. She received her BA from Auburn and an MA from the University of Illinois, Urbana. After serving from 1960 until 1964 as an archivist for the State of Illinois, she became Director of Research for the Illinois Civil War Centennial Commission. She has just completed a term as a member of the council of the Society of American Archivists. Among several publications is *Eighty Years at Hull House* which she co-edited with Allen F. Davis. At present she is the editor of the Jane Addams Papers project being carried out at the University of Illinois, Chicago.

Clark W. Nelson, Archivist of the Mayo Foundation, completed graduate and undergraduate work in history and archival administration at Brigham Young University and American University. He is a Fellow of the Society of American Archivists; technical notes editor of *The American Archivist;* and has served as chairman and member of SAA committees concerned with archival preservation.

Robert Rosenthal is the Curator of Special Collections in the University of Chicago Library. He also teaches courses in rare books as well as manuscript and archival curatorship. He is a graduate of Indiana University and the University of Chicago.